Acorns and Archangels

" GOD'S
RICHES
AT
CHRIST'S
EXPENSE "

Acorns and Archangels

Resources for Ordinary Time

(The Feast of the Transfiguration to All Hallows')

Ruth Burgess

WILD GOOSE PUBLICATIONS
www.ionabooks.com

Contents of book © the individual contributors
Compilation © 2009 Ruth Burgess

First published 2009 by
Wild Goose Publications, 4th Floor, Savoy House, 140 Sauchiehall St, Glasgow G2 3DH, UK.
Wild Goose Publications is the publishing division of the Iona Community.
Scottish Charity No. SCO03794. Limited Company Reg. No. SCO96243.
www.ionabooks.com
ISBN 978-1-905010-56-1

Cover painting and internal illustration © Scott Riley

The publishers gratefully acknowledge the support of the Drummond Trust,
3 Pitt Terrace, Stirling FK8 2EY in producing this book.

Overseas distribution:
Australia: Willow Connection Pty Ltd, Unit 4A, 3-9 Kenneth Road, Manly Vale, NSW 2093
New Zealand: Pleroma, Higginson Street, Otane 4170, Central Hawkes Bay
Canada: Novalis/Bayard Publishing & Distribution, 10 Lower Spadina Ave., Suite 400,
Toronto, Ontario M5V 2Z2

Printed by Bell & Bain, Thornliebank, Glasgow

GENERAL CONTENTS

CONTENTS IN DETAIL

Key to symbols	
✝	Prayer
✜	Biblical reflection
☡	Liturgy
♫	Song
☚	Story
▥	Sermon
🎭	Script
♥	Meditation
▥	Reflection
✗	Poem
⛰	Creed

Key to symbols	
✟	Prayer
✣	Biblical reflection
☒	Liturgy
♫	Song
🐟	Story
📖	Sermon
🎭	Script
♥	Meditation
▦	Reflection
✗	Poem
⛪	Creed

Key to symbols	
✠	Prayer
✤	Biblical reflection
✍	Liturgy
♫	Song
✍	Story
📖	Sermon
🎭	Script
♥	Meditation
▦	Reflection
✻	Poem
⛰	Creed

Key to symbols	
✟	Prayer
⁘	Biblical reflection
♘	Liturgy
♫	Song
☖	Story
📖	Sermon
😀	Script
♥	Meditation
⊞	Reflection
✈	Poem
⛰	Creed

For Val and for Ted
and for the congregation of St Vincent's Church, Whitburn.
With thanks and love

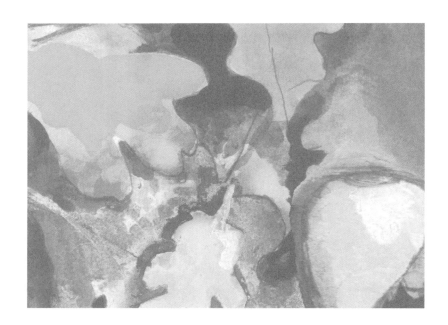

INTRODUCTION

Acorns and Archangels is a resource book which covers the period from the Feast of the Transfiguration (August 6th) to All Hallows' Eve (October 31st). This period is usually referred to as Ordinary Time, or the days after Trinity.

It is the final book in a series of resource books that cover the Christian calendar★. I didn't set out to create a series, but the material kept coming in!

This book contains material relating to the psalms and the prophets, the gospels (after the Transfiguration), and the Acts of the Apostles and New Testament letters. There are also women's stories, sections on saints and angels and harvest, a variety of blessings and a play for Hallowe'en.

The material in this book consists of the stuff that liturgies are made of: stories, songs, responses, poems, scripts, biblical reflections, sermons and prayers.

My grateful thanks to all the contributors for the wealth of rich material I have been privileged to edit – it's been a labour of surprise and delight. It's also been the second time that one book has turned into two!

Thanks are also due, as always, to the staff of Wild Goose Publications for their professionalism, creativity and support: Sandra Kramer, Jane Darroch Riley, Alex O'Neill, Neil Paynter and Lorna Rae Sutton. What a team! Particular thanks to Neil for his loving care and attention to detail. Thanks also to Scott Riley for his artwork.

God of the seasons,
you surround us with beauty and wonder:
you smile in the ripening fruit,
you dance in the tumbling leaves.

Teach us to dance with you,
to act justly
and to share fairly,
to love you in friend and stranger
all the moments of our nights and days.

Ruth Burgess, August 2008

★ *Candles & Conifers: Resources for All Saints' and Advent*
Hay & Stardust: Resources for Christmas to Candlemas
Eggs and Ashes: Practical & Liturgical Resources for Lent and Holy Week
Fire and Bread: Resources for Easter Day to Trinity Sunday
Bare Feet and Buttercups: Resources for Ordinary Time – Trinity Sunday to the Feast of the Transfiguration
Acorns and Archangels: Resources for Ordinary Time – Feast of the Transfiguration to All Hallows'

THE FEAST OF THE TRANSFIGURATION

TRANSFIGURATION

This is my son:
there are no screaming teenagers
no adoring fans
nor desperate followers,
no wired, dark-besuited heavies
no, not here
no trappings.

This is my son:
no red carpet laid down
only on this lonely path
wine,
wounds,
blood.

This is my son:
no flash photographers
only the one spotlight
but in this spot – what light.

Penelope Hewlett

TRANSFIGURATION: A DISCIPLE REFLECTS

(based on Luke 9:28–42)

Did we mind when Jesus took them
with him up the mountain?
Not really. We were used to it, you see.
Peter, James and John – and Jesus:
the inner circle. The kernel of the kingdom,
if you like. And so the rest of us
got on with things at ground level,
serving the Servant of the Lord
in whatever ways we could.

But it was Jesus people came to see,
and who could blame them – so did we.
This time though it felt different.
They were away for ages for a start.
Not just another early morning
praying in the hills. They were gone
a couple of days at least.
When they came back down
they were different, all of them.

Jesus was quietly radiant.
The others? Well, they seemed ... subdued;
almost in shock.
They didn't say a word about it
till some time later.
I suppose it didn't help
what they came back to:
the rest of us in disarray,
unable to heal a child.

So what did Jesus say?
Reproach? No, sorrow more like,
at a faithless generation.
He stepped in as usual,
taking our unbelief into
his extraordinary understanding
of the love of God.
Seeing that healing happen
was like a mountaintop experience.
Awesome!

Carol Dixon

A SERVICE FOR HIROSHIMA DAY

(6 August: the Feast of the Transfiguration)

Call to worship

Then Jesus came and stood among them. 'Peace be with you,' he said.
After saying this, he showed them his hands and his side.
The disciples were filled with joy at seeing the Lord.
Jesus said to them again, 'Peace be with you.' (John 20:19–21)

In the name of Jesus Christ, I say, 'Peace be with you'
PEACE BE WITH YOU
Peace to you who are nearby and to those who are far off
PEACE BE WITH YOU
Peace to friend and to enemy
PEACE BE WITH YOU
Let us worship God

Song

Prayer of repentance

O Christ, true image of God
WE COME, DRAWN BY YOUR GLORY
O Christ, revealer of life in its fullness
WE HIDE, FEARFUL OF YOUR LIGHT OF TRUTH
O Christ, lifted up in weakness
WE HOPE IN YOUR POWER FOR CHANGE

Because on this day ... years ago, a great flash was seen,
not to reveal the divine image but to incinerate it in a multitude of God's children:
and light is become darkness,
God weeps ...... *silence*
Lord have mercy
CHRIST HAVE MERCY

Because people are whispering, and terror is everywhere,
security is become fear and fear is become death:
and what was open is covered up,
God weeps ...... *silence*
Lord have mercy
CHRIST HAVE MERCY

Because children lie bleeding from great wounds that gape in their throats and sides,
in the cities they disappear without trace, as if they had never been,
and innocence is become corruption,
God weeps ...... *silence*
Lord have mercy
CHRIST HAVE MERCY

Because women are beaten, raped and degraded,
commodified and trafficked, attacked through their children,
and tenderness is become weakness,
God weeps ...... *silence*
Lord have mercy
CHRIST HAVE MERCY

Because lakes are poisoned and air and forests burn and choke
to feed the insatiable appetites of jaded palates,
and creation is become destruction,
God weeps ...... *silence*
Lord have mercy
CHRIST HAVE MERCY

Because weapons are bought and sold in the marketplace as easily as onions,
armies mass on borders and killing comes lightly everywhere,
and peace is become war,
God weeps ...... *silence*
Lord have mercy
CHRIST HAVE MERCY

Because we cry, 'peace, peace'
but there is no peace in Jerusalem,
and life is become death,
God weeps ...... *silence*
Lord have mercy
CHRIST HAVE MERCY

O Christ our true peace,
who felt the desolation of death
and the fear of abandonment,
deliver us who also recognise the shape of desolation
and weep.

Preserve us from the fear that makes us vicious,
give us insight to see the structures of injustice by which we profit,

and grace to cherish all people in our vulnerability,
knowing that we all live within your love.
AMEN

Silence

Scripture reading: James 3:17–18

For the Word of God in scripture
for the Word of God among us
for the Word of God within us
THANKS BE TO GOD

Scripture reading: Mark 9:2–8
followed by a sung hallelujah

Response to the Word

Planting olive trees (or another symbolic peace act). An introduction to the significance of the olive tree as a sign of peace, and also its economic significance in the Middle East, should be given here. While the planting happens, the people sing:

'Ya Rabba ssalami' (*We Will Walk His Way*, John L. Bell, Wild Goose Publications, 2008), or another chant

Tending the trees of peace

People are invited to spend a few minutes sharing thoughts about how they can tend the tree of peace in their own situations.

Song of invocation: 'Almighty God'(*Love and Anger*, John L. Bell and Graham Maule, Wild Goose Publications, 1997)

Prayers of intercession

For fullness of life, we give thanks, O God,
and as we pray for ourselves,
we pray for all people, made in your image
to know life in all its fullness.
FOR THE TREE OF PEACE HAS ITS ROOTS IN JUSTICE

Here follow intercessions from different situations of conflict, each petition finishing with the words:

Lord Jesus, that they may know life in all its fullness
FOR THE TREE OF PEACE HAS ITS ROOTS IN JUSTICE

Lord Jesus,
may we who love you, and find in you our hope,
bear witness, as Thomas did,
that your risen body still carries the marks
of the world's violence, injustice and greed,
and as we remember,
help us to keep faith with all who still, today,
suffer the outrages of violence, injustice and greed.
In our actions, in our prayers, in our choices and in our commitment,
make us makers of peace and your faithful children.
AMEN

Blessing

Peace between nations
Peace between neighbours
Peace between person and person
In love of the God of life.
THE PEACE OF CHRIST ABOVE ALL PEACE.
LET US GO IN PEACE.

Sharing of peace

People greet one another with a sign of peace.

Sending song: 'The peace of the earth be with you'
(*Church Hymnary 4*, Canterbury Press, John L. Bell, ed.)

Kathy Galloway

GOD OF LIGHT AND GLORY

God of light and glory,
we look at the world you have created and we rejoice.
We rejoice in the sunshine and the storms of summer,
the taste of berries freshly picked,
the scent of roses and lavender,
the feel of warm grass under our feet.
In the face of all the busyness that crowds our living,
keep us attentive to the beauty around us,
fashioned and illuminated by your love.

God of light and glory,
we look at the way we live in the world and we weep.
We weep for the destruction of Hiroshima and Nagasaki in 1945.
For the fighting in Israel and Palestine, Lebanon, Iraq and Afghanistan today.
For the loss of life and the loss of trust,
for our fallen, broken humanity
and our persistence in pursuing our own interests
at the expense of our neighbours' needs.
Through the darkness and the tears of those who are wounded,
bereaved, afraid,
shine your healing, restoring light.

God of light and glory,
we remember before you those we know who are in need.
We think of those who are in nursing homes, hospitals and hospices
and of those who care for them.
We think of the emergency services,
the coastguard and the mountain rescue teams
who come to our aid when our pastimes falter and turn to pain.
Strengthen and comfort them with your loving presence.

God of light and glory,
we thank you above all that in Jesus you have revealed yourself to us,
and that through the Holy Spirit you are with us still,
a lamp shining in a dark place,
until the day dawns
and the morning star rises in our hearts. Amen

Cally Booker

THE DAY WE WENT TO PITLOCHRY

The day we went to Pitlochry
it was a day of light.
Sunlight playing on ferns and woodland clover
was a dancing sprite
almost tangible yet elusively, mischievously ethereal.
I was glad to be alone.
The children, eager to find Ossian's Cave, had run ahead.
Glancing at a tree I experienced transformation.
For a moment the sun illumined
an intricate chain of spider webs,
stretched from branch to branch,
and hung with dazzle-drops of rain.
My being brimmed delight and glory and praise.

The moment passed.
The tree, veiling its surprising secret, receded in the shade
and I tiptoed away, cradling stillness within.

Reaching the Hermitage I looked out on rocks,
listened to the tumbling river
and felt this place well-chosen
and an affinity with the hermit, long dead, who'd lived here.

Going home two rainbows hung, archways in our path,
and as Julian dissected and lectured on refracted light,
Katy and Paul dreamt of pots of gold
and I of covenant and promise and hope.

Next day, at Mass, the gospel was of Christ's Transfiguration.
I knew how Peter, James and John felt,
graced and privileged and only half understanding
the secret, hidden spirit of light
that made Him who He was.

And I thought of the spark within us all
that awaits the shimmering, shining moments of love.

Mary Hanrahan

JESUS TRANSFIGURED

(Mark 9:2–8)

They climbed a hill together,
Jesus and Peter, James and John,
to find a quiet place,
a place apart from the crowds
who were clamouring for healing,
and for Jesus to teach them more about the kingdom of heaven.

The demands on them had been heavy.
He had fed the hungry crowd,
healed the deaf and the blind,
and raised the little daughter of Jairus who they thought was dead.
He had taught them such unusual things,
always surprising them with his stories,
and they began to wonder who he could be.
Who could do such things?
Heal as he did?
Speak such wise words in the synagogue?

And then in the quiet of that place
they began to see him differently.
They recognised that in some mysterious way
Jesus was the Son of God;
the one for whom they had waited and longed,
just as the prophets of old had waited and longed for the Messiah.

They did not understand quite what was happening,
but gradually, and oh so slowly,
they began to see that they must listen to Jesus
and learn from him,
for what he was teaching would change the world.

After this encounter with mystery,
they returned down the hill,
back to the ordinary,
back to the waiting crowds
and other requests for healing,
and answers to the question:
'Who is this man?'

Who is this man?
How do I listen and understand and respond to his teaching?

Let me find a quiet place, a place apart,
and try to enter into the mystery,
that I, too, might have a moment of recognition
and of knowing and of travelling deeper into mystery.

'This is my Son, my beloved; listen to him.'
Let me receive these words into my heart
that my life might be changed.

Lynda Wright

THEMA

(a short story of transfiguration)

Thema was 20. She was tall, slim, attractive, with a light-brown skin, inherited from her white British mother and her black West African father. She always appeared in jeans and trainers, T-shirt and fleece. Well, you do when you're young. And doesn't everyone more or less when staying for a week on Iona?

Thema's mother, Elizabeth, had gone to work in West Africa, had met and fallen in love with a man there. They had married, and had children, but Elizabeth's husband died, and she returned with the children to live in the north of England. However, she always made sure that the children were aware of their West African heritage.

Thema was 21 that week, and when she came into the refectory for breakfast that birthday morning – wow! Everyone was absolutely amazed and struck dumb! What a transformation! Not that day the jeans, T-shirt and fleece! Thema was dressed in African robes, all yellow and green, including the tall turban on her head. Suddenly she looked so African, so 'other'. She was still the Thema folk knew, but that day she looked every inch an African princess.

One thing was for sure, folk certainly saw Thema in a different light that day!

David Hamflett

PROPHETS AND KINGS

SALES PITCH

(Numbers 22)

Would I lie to you?
I ask.
Would I lie to you?
This donkey can talk.
I heard it myself.
Well, almost.

You know Big Abe?
(he's as honest as the day is long) –
his son Joel has a mate
who was actually there when it happened.
This prophet Balaam had been summoned
to put a curse on us.
Up he rides on this very donkey
ready to do the dirty deed.
But she won't cooperate;
turns off the road into a field,
walks into a wall,
lies down and won't get up.
So Balaam starts to lay into her with his staff
and she looks straight at him and says:
'What's with the corporal punishment, squire?
What have I done to deserve it?
How many years have you been riding on my back?
Have I made a habit of this?
Have you considered that there might be a logical explanation
for my apparently aberrant behaviour?'
And Balaam looks up
and sees this angel blocking the road.
Big feller,
drawn sword,
not looking too happy.
'Little man,' says he.
'You are lucky to be alive.
Had your donkey gone a few steps further
I would have ended your miserable existence.
But I would have spared her.'
So this little beast not only spoke,
but saved the man's life.

Well,
no,
I can't absolutely guarantee
that she'll speak to you.
But it's a good story,
isn't it?
Worth a pint.

Brian Ford

SOMETHING APPROACHING A PRAYER

Er ......
Um ......
Yahweh.
I believe that is your name,
although I'm told that,
for reasons that I cannot grasp,
your worshippers won't speak your name out loud.
If you were one of our gods I'd know what to do:
bring an offering to the priests
and they would graciously pass on my message.
I believe your lot do something similar.
But I have nothing to offer.
Absolutely
nothing.
And I suppose I can hardly expect
the god of the Israelites to listen
to a citizen of the stinking heap of still burning rubble
formerly known as the city of Jericho.
But they believe that you made the whole universe,
and that you are a god of justice and compassion.
So how come your lot massacred every inhabitant,
including my wife and children,
and destroyed every building,
including the business I'd worked for twenty years to build up?
I only survived because I was away on a trading trip;
most of the time I wish I hadn't.
I suppose our lot would have done exactly the same to the Israelites
if we'd won.
And it could be argued that a quick death is preferable

to a life of drudgery as a slave.
And yet ......
And yet ......
Why?
That's all I want to know, Yahweh.
Why?

Brian Ford

GOSSIP ABOUT SPIES

(Joshua 1:1–24)

And what were they doing in a place like that
may I ask?
Two good Jewish boys,
they had a job to do.

I can guess:
Day's work done,
time for some fun.
Well, they nearly paid very dearly for it,
didn't they?

And what right had they to promise
that she and her household would be saved?
And Joshua agreed!
And some of our boys had to be diverted from their Yahweh-given duties
to take care of them.

What sort of religion saves whores?
Eh?

Brian Ford

THOSE ON THE MARGINS*

God of Rahab and Joshua,
God of those on the margins,
we pray for our world:
for the people you show goodness to,
for the people you show goodness through –
the unlikely people – the marginal people.
People like Joshua, a tentative leader of a ragged nation chosen
to bring God's glory to light in the world;
people like Rahab, a prostitute whose act of self-preservation
helped God to restore Israel's fortunes;
people from the margins whom God brought in ...

We pray for the marginal people known to us today:
those worried about their lives,
those concerned about their future,
those who don't feel at home in the place they now live,
those of our community who are hurting today.
From the margins bring them in, O Lord, and in your mercy
HEAR OUR PRAYER.

We pray for the marginal people in our land:
those driven by poverty to sell themselves, to steal or to deal in
deadly drugs,
those struggling to find decent work or any work at all,
those who bring up families alone,
those who live lives that are the object of society's censure.
From the margins bring them in, O Lord, and in your mercy
HEAR OUR PRAYER.

We pray for the marginal people of the world:
for those displaced by war in ...
for those who need land and food in ...
for those hoping for peace in ...
From the margins bring them in, O Lord, and in your mercy
HEAR OUR PRAYER.

Bring them in, O Lord,
all those outside of power,
all those deprived of peace.
Bring them in, with our help,
for this is the work you have placed into our hands.

And faced with the awesome responsibility of this work, bring us in too,
right in
to love and serve you
with joyful obedience in the life of your world.

MERCIFUL LORD,
ACCEPT THESE PRAYERS
FOR THE SAKE OF YOUR SON,
OUR SAVIOUR, JESUS CHRIST. AMEN

John Davies

* Intercessions with reference to the story of Rahab and Joshua (Joshua 1:1–24)

THE SONG OF DEBORAH

(Judges 5:1–31)

(Tune: Love unknown)

Deborah:
I sing a bold new song,
a song of victory,
the battle has been won
and Israel is set free.
Hear me, O kings,
as I proclaim
the Lord is God,
to him I sing.

Jael:
My song begins in fear
as armies rage around,
it ends triumphantly
when Israel's trumpets sound.
But on my floor
a stain of blood
remains to tell
the price of war.

Sisera's mother:
My song is hard to sing:
I sing it in my pain,
the pain of mother's love
which weeps, and waits in vain.
Can I believe
that he's delayed
by spoils of war,
or should I grieve?

Deborah:
I sing a song of joy
for peace now newly gained,
the caravans return,
the God of Israel reigns.
Both rich and poor
rejoice today,
musicians play
to praise the Lord.

Cally Booker

SONG OF RUTH

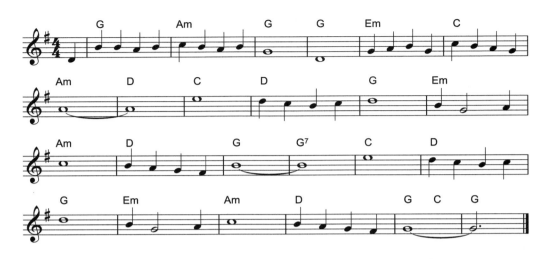

Entreat me not to leave you or forsake you,
let me follow you along the way.
Your people shall be my people,
and your God shall be my God.
Your people shall be my people,
and your God shall be my God.

Do not send me back to where I came from,
to a life of darkness with no hope.
Your people shall be my people,
and your God shall be my God.
Your people shall be my people,
and your God shall be my God.

Let me walk with you along the pathway,
even though the road is long and hard.
Your people shall be my people,
and your God shall be my God.
Your people shall be my people,
and your God shall be my God.

Carol Dixon

WHO WERE THEY?

Ruth. The foreigner, the widow, the faithful one, the naive one, the wily one, the seductress, the manoeuvred one, the brazen hussy, the one who put her trust in Israel's God?

Naomi. The mother, the widow, the sad one, the bereft one, the crafty one, the manipulator, the matchmaker, the one who longed for grandchildren, the one with a cunning plan?

Boaz. The kind farmer, the rich and generous one, the powerful one, the startled one, the keeper of the Commandments, the one who saw what he fancied and went for it and reaped his reward?

And as for what went on
in the dark
under the covers
on the threshing floor
next to the heap of corn,
who knows?

God knows.

And God blessed them with Obed

O for organised by his granny
B for beloved by his daddy
E for embraced by his mummy
D for dreamed of and delighted in by God.

Amen

Ruth Burgess

A STORY FROM 1ST SAMUEL

(Chapter 16)

God told Samuel the prophet that one of Jesse's sons would be the next King of Israel.
So Samuel went to see Jesse.

Jesse called each of his sons, one by one, before Samuel.

First his eldest son.
Samuel thought, this boy is tall and strong. He would rule Israel well.
But God said to Samuel, 'No, this is not the one I choose.'

The second son was very honest and clever.
Samuel thought, this man would rule justly.
But God said to Samuel, 'No, this is not the one I choose.'

The third son was holy. He prayed every day.
Samuel thought, perhaps this is the man whom God had chosen.
But again, God said to Samuel, 'No, this is not the one I choose.'

Jesse's fourth son was a warrior, he could have led Israel into battle;
another son was polite and would have made a good diplomat;
another managed people wisely;
but each time God said to Samuel, 'No, this is not the one I choose.'

Samuel said to Jesse, 'Haven't you any more sons?'
Jesse answered him: 'Well, there is my youngest son, David,
but he's just a boy.
He's only old enough to be minding the sheep.'

So David was sent for.
He was healthy and good-looking and he had a twinkle in his eye.
And God said to Samuel, 'This is the one, make him king.'

And God said to Samuel, 'You see, I do not judge as you judge.
I am not interested in how strong people look,
or how sensible they seem to be.
I look at what people are like inside.
I look at what they value and what makes them who they are.'

Ruth Burgess

Note: This was written to be dramatised.

I SAID NO

(Esther 1)

Listen to me,
women of 127 provinces
women from everywhere.

Listen to me,
women of every tribe and time,
listen to my story.

I broke the mould.
I said no to a man.
I disobeyed my husband.

If I had not been the queen
my words and actions
would have been punished and forgotten,
I would have been silenced.

But because I was the queen
I was heard and noticed.
The king was furious.

He consulted his advisors.

His advisors decided that
they did not want me as
a role model for their wives.

I was dismissed.
A younger, more beautiful woman
was groomed to take my place.

The king sent a message to every province
stating that
husbands, in their own homes, must be respected by their wives.

Listen to me,
women of every province,
of all ages;
I send you a message too:

Women must be respected by their husbands,
in their own homes and in society.

Respect and love
cannot be imposed by anyone.
They need a mutual space in which to grow.

My words and my actions
cost me my crown,
but I retained my integrity.

When you hear the story of Esther,
remember my story too.
I am Vashti.

Ruth Burgess

ON THE ROAD

(Isaiah 35)

On the road
there are shadows
and raindrops
reeds and flowers
and the twinkling of stars.

On the road
there are friends
there are strangers.
You will need to ask questions
understand new ideas.

On the road
there is sand
and fresh water
high hills
maybe caves.

On the road there are gifts:
strength for the weary
forgiveness for the sinner
hope for the sad.

At the road end
there is welcome and wonder
food and drink
home and singing.
There is shouting for joy.

Ruth Burgess

DO NOT FEAR, MY DEAR ONE

(Based on Isaiah 44:1–5)

Do not fear, my dear one, my child.
I know you.
I knew you when you were still in the womb.

I have held your hopes and dreams in my hands.
I have laughed with you in the good times, the glad times.
I have smiled with delight when life is abundant.

I will never leave you.

I have wrapped my arms around you when your hopes
have been dashed and your dreams shattered.
I have held you close when fear and uncertainty
have filled your horizons.
I have wept when your tears flowed freely for what
you had lost.

I will never leave you.

I will be there, in good times and bad.
I will refresh you with water in times of drought.
I will pour streams of love and hope and promise
in times of emptiness and need.

I will help your new shoots to grow,
like willows growing beside flowing streams.

Kareen Lowther

I HAVE CALLED YOU BY NAME

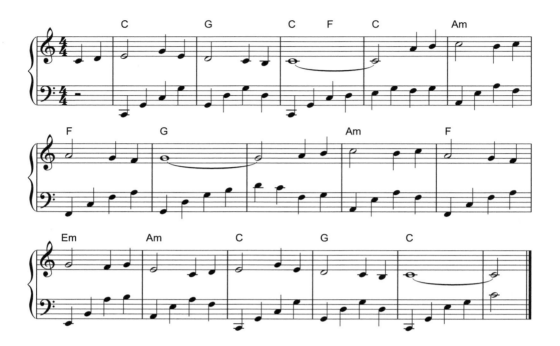

'I have called you by name,' says the Lord,
'I have called you by name, you are mine,
I have called you by name, I have called you by name,
I have called you by name, you are mine.'

'I have given you life,' says the Lord,
'I have given you life, you are mine,
I have given you life, I have given you life,
I have given you life, you are mine.'

'You're the joy of my heart,' says the Lord,
'you're the joy of my heart, you are mine,
you're the joy of my heart, you're the joy of my heart,
you're the joy of my heart, you are mine.'

Carol Dixon

FRIENDS

Three friends in a fiery furnace ...
Shadrach, Meshach and Abednego,
having a flaming good time.

Three friends.
Staying together when things got hot.
Prepared to die together
in a fiery furnace
for friendship and for faith.

Three friends,
with a burning desire to go all the way
for righteousness and truth.

Three?
No ... more ...
For in the midst of friendship and of faith,
in the burning heat of sacrifice,
God came,
and love and faith and truth were not consumed
by hatred's fire.
And three became four,
and mystery became truth
and flames lost their power
over friendship and true faith.

Three friends –
bound to each other and to God,
on fire with all that's good,
offering what was right –
that even some old fiery furnace
could not consume.

Three friends in a fiery furnace ...
Shadrach, Meshach and Abednego,
having a flaming good time.

Tom Gordon

TO BE A DANIEL

'Dare to be a Daniel', I sang as a child –
lustily!
'Dare to stand alone', I was assured was a good thing to do –
often!
But it was all very well for them to say,
these grown-ups
who knew nothing of child bullying
and cared less, it appeared.
Standing alone just caused more trouble;
being the only one who went to church
just increased the bullying;
being little, and not very brave,
just made it worse;
being convinced that it was best to do things right,
to behave,
to be a credit to the family
just made life more and more lonely.
'Dare to stand alone',
I was assured was a good thing to do –
too often ...
But no one said it would be this hard.
'Dare to be a Daniel,' I sang –
tentatively,
and wondered why ...

'Dare to be a Daniel', I now believe to be right,
often!
'Dare to stand alone' is a good thing to do,
often!
For very well I've learned
from examples of those who've put their life on the line
for principles,
and justice,
and freedom,
and peace.
Standing alone caused more trouble,
more trouble for the authorities
who would seek to silence protest;
to silence the little people, and the not-very-brave
who changed the world

because they stood up to evil and injustice;
to silence those who were convinced that there was a better way,
a way of love,
and gave their lives for the cause.
'Dare to stand alone' was their thing to do –
often,
even when it was unbelievably hard.
'Dare to be a Daniel,' they would sing –
lustily,
and without asking 'Why?'

'Dare to be a Daniel' is a voice which still sings its truth –
often, often ...
'Dare to stand alone' has oft times had its place for me.
And that is all very well for me to say,
now grown up,
understanding all too well a broken world
and caring more, thank God.
Standing alone for troubled causes
and finding others standing with you
just increases the resolve;
being little people, standing up to big forces,
just makes it so necessary;
of course it's best to stand for what is right,
no need to be popular
when you're a credit to humanity
and the lonely and exploited who can't speak for themselves.
'Dare to stand alone'.
Yes, I've done it like Daniel, and I'll do it again –
often!
And it's when it's hardest that it's most important.
'Dare to be a Daniel,' I still sing –
lustily –
and God knows why.

Tom Gordon

JONAH

One day Jonah was sitting down, when God spoke to him and said, 'Jonah, go to the city of Nineveh and tell the people to stop being bad and turn over a new leaf or I will destroy the city and kill everyone.'

Jonah decided to argue so he said, 'God, I will not go today because it's not the weather for travelling, and even if I did go, you would probably not do it and make me look a right fool.'

God was angry, and said, 'Jonah. Go!'

Jonah saw that he had better shut up.

He walked to Joppa in the hot sun and he was getting very cross. He decided he would not go to Nineveh. He would get on a boat and go somewhere else and hide.

Jonah went below to his cabin and was so tired he fell asleep. The ship sailed well for a while and then all of a sudden there began a terrible storm. The captain was getting worried so he ordered everyone to pray to their gods. He went downstairs to wake Jonah up, and when he told Jonah what had happened Jonah told the captain what he'd done. Jonah told the captain to throw him overboard. The captain would not. The captain told Jonah to pray. Jonah did, but nothing happened, so Jonah was thrown overboard.

Jonah was floating on his back when he was swallowed by a whale. He was very cold inside the whale so Jonah prayed to God to let him out. This God did. Jonah was pleased and prayed to God thanking him. Jonah went straight to the city of Nineveh and told everyone the message. At first nobody believed him and they all laughed at him, but there was something about this man that changed their minds. The message got to the king and he told everyone to change their ways. Within forty days, this everyone did. So God forgave them and everyone was happy, except for Jonah.

Jonah was complaining, 'What was the good of me coming? I knew you wouldn't do it. It never happened. Now I'm going to sit here and die.'

God heard this and made a tree grow near Jonah. For a day Jonah sat in the shade of the tree. The next day the tree withered up and died.

Jonah was very unhappy and said, 'Why did that tree wither up and die, I liked it?'

God said to Jonah, 'You feel sorry for that tree like I did for those people.'

Jonah saw God's point and got up and went home happily.

Christopher, aged 10

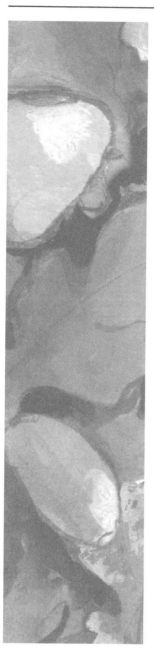

MICAH 6:8

Show love,
act justly,
walk humbly with God:

enough challenge
and adventure

enough wonder
and creativity

enough tears
and laughter

enough task
for a lifetime

enough company
and direction,
to see us safe home.

Ruth Burgess

MICAH 6

Carol Dixon

PSALMS AND WISDOM

A JOB PROFILE

Tested by Satan, so we're led to believe,
you stood firm.
Now, that's quite something!
How did you manage to face down the Devil
and survive?

You lost your children and your wealth,
and you didn't buckle.
Now, that's astonishing!
How did you manage to cope with grief and loss
and keep going?

Friends came and gave you false comfort,
and you kept up the dialogue.
Now, that's incredible!
How did you stay patient with their myriad of words
and not explode?

You broke your silence and complained to God –
and still believed.
Now, that's quite marvellous!
How could you be angry and believing at the same time –
and not lose faith?

And, in the end, you praised the wisdom of your God
and trusted all the more.
Now, that's fantastic!
How could you come through all this
and live?

Stand with me, Job,
as I try to survive the devil's wily ways.
Walk with me, Job,
as I seek comfort in my loss and grief.
Sit with me, Job,
as I need to be patient with my false comforters.
Wait with me, Job,
as I struggle to make sense of the anger and belief of my faith.
Stay with me, Job,
as I find new wisdom in your God – and mine.

Tom Gordon

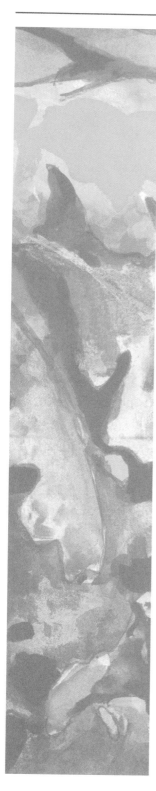

23RD

Sinking in a sea
of stress and success,
you buoy me
with your living waters
until I am at peace;

running down
endless corridors
to never-ending meetings,
you detour me
to the pathways
leading to your joy;

stumbling through
the thorn bushes
of a culture which seeks
to tear my soul to shreds,
you prepare a picnic
in the garden of grace;

famished and peckish
from wandering
the shadows of sin and death,
you fill me
with sweet-tasting hope;

fleeing
the very life
I convince myself
I am seeking,
you slow me down
so goodness and mercy
can catch up with me

and push me
into your heart.

Thom M Shuman

I'M ALIVE TODAY

I'm alive today.
The care of God will guide me.
God is strong and he can lift me up.
The strongness of God will look after me.
God is wise and he can teach me.
God can tell me what to say.
God shows me the way of life.
God tells me when my enemies are here.
God is looking, God is listening all the time.
God knows the way that I am going, he tells me when I'm bad.
God watches over me and God listens to me.
Holy Spirit be in my speaking.
You hear me everywhere, on earth from heaven.
Help me from getting into trouble.

A class of seven-year-olds reflecting on the twenty-third psalm

PSALM 40:1–11

Tune: Bugeilio'r Gwenith Gwyn (Watching the Wheat)

For the Lord I waited long,
he stooped to hear my crying.
He pulled me from the clinging mire
and from the chasm saved me;
now my feet stand on a rock,
he makes me walk in safety;
he put a new song in my mouth
in praise of God my Saviour.

Those who see what God has done
are filled with awe and wonder;
how happy those who trust the Lord
and do not turn to idols.
Dear Lord God, how much you've done,
how wonderful your plans are.
You put a new song in my mouth
in praise of God my Saviour.

When you called I answered you,
'I'm here, Lord, I am listening';
you ask me not for sacrifice
but for ears that are open;
I delight to do your will,
my heart guards your commandments.
You put a new song in my mouth
in praise of God my Saviour.

Margaret Harvey

PSALM 91

(Tune: Ebenezer)

Those who live in God's own shelter,
in his shadow find their rest,
say to him, 'You are my refuge,
God, in whom I put my trust.'
He will keep you safe from danger,
rescued from the fowler's snare.
He will spread his great wings over you,
you'll find safety in his care.

With his truth as shield and buckler
no night terrors shall you fear,
daytime's arrows shall not pierce you,
plague nor evil shall come near;
though a thousand fall beside you,
thousands fall at your right hand,
though you look with fear and wonder
yet with God, secure you'll stand.

When you make God your defender
evil shall not touch your home,
angels keep their guard about you
lest you fall against a stone;
you shall tread upon the serpent
lions trample underfoot;
when you call, then God will answer,
he will fill your life with good.

Margaret Harvey

PSALM 116

(Tune: All through the night)

I love God because he listens,
he hears my prayer,
every time I call out to him
he hears my prayer;
danger crowded all around me,
fear of death did overwhelm me,
then I cried to God for safety,
he heard my prayer.

Full of mercy and compassion
this is our God;
the protector of the helpless
this is our God;
I was brought low but he saved me.
Be at rest my soul within me.
God has been so good towards me,
this is my God.

You have saved me from destruction,
you heard my prayer,
dried my tears and stopped my weeping,
you heard my prayer,
you have rescued me from stumbling;
daily in your presence walking,
Lord, my God, I live rejoicing.
You hear my prayer.

Margaret Harvey

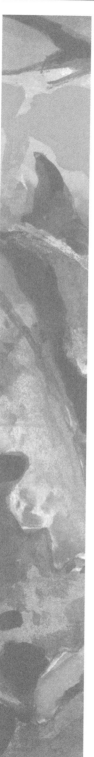

I AM A TRAVELLER ON THE EARTH

(Psalm 119:111)

I am a traveller on the earth,
wandering, exploring,
foot after foot over bamboo leaves,
brown earth, broken plank;
I am a traveller on the earth,
swimming and diving,
searching for coral.

I am a traveller on the earth,
bumping and jolting,
along earthen airstrip,
through rut and dip,
up to Amani.

I am a traveller on the earth,
stepping and balancing,
over roots and branches,
along broken bridge,
over puddle and storm drain.

I am a traveller on the earth,
smelling and tasting,
seduced by pepper,
mangostani and cinnamon,
sipping tamarind juice with lemon slice.

I am a traveller on the earth,
feeling and burning;
warm air caresses my skin,
hot sun burns my back,
the night air buzzes with life.
I am a traveller on the earth,
feeling and burning,
in darkness and in sunshine.

I am a traveller on the earth,
sheltering and waiting,
through storm and in heat,
through mud and rain,
in darkness and in sunshine.

I am a traveller on the earth,
giving and taking,
praying and hoping,
seeing pleading eyes
and outstretched hands,
unfinished buildings
and donkey carts.

I am a traveller on the earth,
listening and learning,
to refugees' stories
grieving parent,
the man with AIDS.

I am a traveller on the earth,
sharing, rejoicing,
a newborn child,
a music scholarship;
I am a traveller on the earth,
listening and learning,
through smiles and greetings.

Judy Dinnen

A poem about travelling in Rwanda and Tanzania in 2002.

PSALM 133

(Tune: Ar lan y môr, Welsh traditional)

How wonderful it is, how pleasant,
to live together as one body:
precious as oil for the anointing,
wonderful to be God's people.

Life-giving as the dew on Hermon
that falls upon the hills of Zion,
God promises to give his blessing,
life eternal to his people.

Margaret Harvey

A CALL TO THE UNIVERSE
(Psalm 148)

In the heights:
sun and moon
armies of angels
shining stars.

In the depths:
earth and oceans
birds and dragons
trees full of fruit.

In the heights:
hail and lightning,
snow and winds,
mists.

In the depths:
men and women,
children, elders,
kings.

A call to the universe,
every plant, every creature –
let us sing our Maker's glory,
let us praise God's name.

A call to the universe –
Hallelujah! Praise God!

Ruth Burgess

PSALM 150

Hallelujah!

Praise God with street rap.
Praise God with Bach cantatas.

Praise God with tattooed hands.
Praise God with arthritic hands.

Praise God with smiling eyes.
Praise God with stuffy noses and pockets filled with hankies.

Praise God in stained-glass sanctuaries.
Praise God in public houses.

Let every living, breathing,
big and tall,
short and small,
beloved creature
praise God!

Hallelujah!

Thom M Shuman

WISDOM IS SUPREME

(Proverbs 4)

Wisdom is supreme – therefore get wisdom.

Living God, with you comes liberating knowledge, in you is deep understanding, from you wisdom shines into our lives.

There are no limits to the areas of life where wisdom can be found. For us, in our daily tasks, often wondering what decision to make, sometimes struggling with our consciences, charged with responsibility to look after others and with demanding tasks of work: good Lord, make us wise.

For those who provide leadership, in our workplaces, in our city, in our country and in our world – having to deal with so many conflicting calls on their interests, having to fight the temptations of power, charged with protecting the weakest while so often drawn towards the influence of the strong: good Lord, make them wise.

For those who face difficulty, those in pain, those whose minds and hearts are weighed down, confused, tired, whose bodies are failing them, who need to know when hope and healing will come: good Lord, make them wise.

Esteem her, and she will exalt you; embrace her, and she will honour you.

May each of us know you walking with us, lifting us, throwing your loving arms around us. May the world be blessed by the spreading of your wisdom. May the earth be healed by the knowledge of your love.

Merciful God, Wisdom's source, accept these prayers, for the sake of Jesus Christ, Wisdom's life. Amen

John Davies

YOU WERE THERE
(Proverbs 8:22–30)

You were there at the beginning
when he was thinking,
planning, making.

You were a child
handing him a paintbrush,
an architect sharing designs.

The two of you
grew up together;
singing, laughing, playing.

You made a world
full of delight.

Ruth Burgess

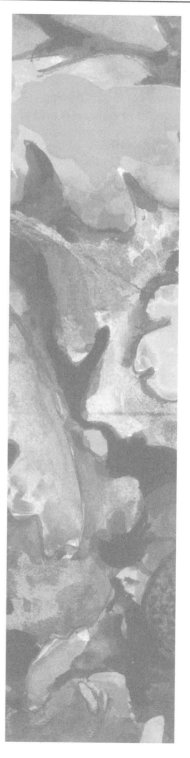

COME WISDOM

(Proverbs 1–8)

Come Wisdom,
breath of God's power,
bringer of goodness and love.

Come Wisdom,
stream of God's glory,
sharer of justice and truth.

Come Wisdom,
light of God's treasure,
gifter of friendship and joy.

Come Wisdom,
meet us in our marketplaces,
keep watch over our lives.

Ruth Burgess

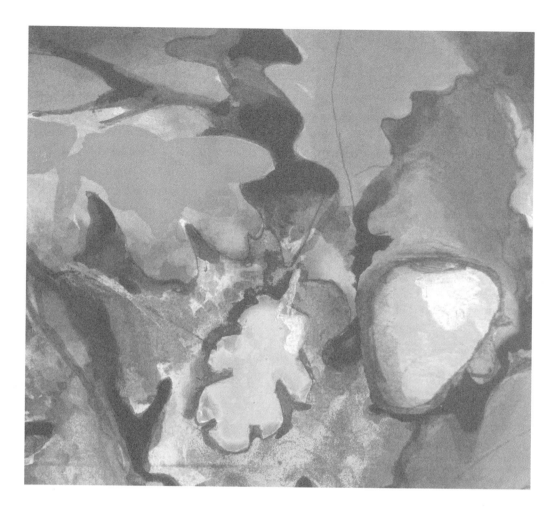

THE WAY OF JESUS

ONE DAY

One day there was a man called Zacchaeus. He was working with his pen and paper. Zacchaeus said to the people pay twelve coins. He gave the Romans ten coins and kept two for himself and put them in his pocket. So he was rich. He had a beautiful house.

One day Jesus came and Zacchaeus wanted to see him, but he had one problem, he was little so he could not see over the people's heads. He saw a tree and climbed up it. Jesus saw him and said, 'What are you doing up there?' Everyone was laughing. Jesus said, 'Get down here, Zacchaeus,' so he got down. Jesus said, 'I am coming to yours for tea.'

Zacchaeus was nervous. He got all his servants to tidy up. They got out all the best knives and forks and spoons and it all looked beautiful. Jesus and Zacchaeus sat at the table and were talking. They drank all the wine and ate the chicken. Zacchaeus said, 'I'm sorry about all of the things I have took off the poor people. I will give them their money back.' Jesus said, 'That's what I want to hear. You have got everything. Sort it out.' Then they finished their tea.

Veronica, aged 8

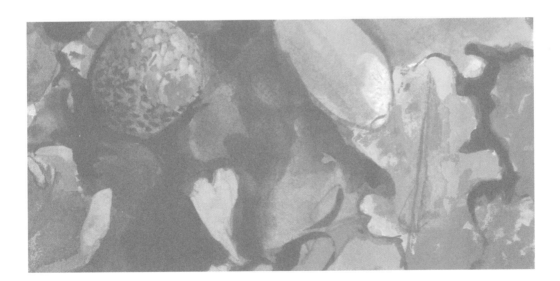

WHERE YOU SIT

We leave our box seats
at the symphony or ballpark,
and pray you won't catch our eye
as we pass you
sitting with the homeless.

We wait for a few minutes
at the doctor's office
to get a $10 shot
so we won't catch the flu,
while half a world away
you sit for a week
hoping medicine,
which will cost you
a year's wages,
finds its way to your village.

We sit in our home theatres,
catching the latest 'reality'
on our plasma screens,
while you sit in the darkness
rocking your child to sleep,
as she cries from the ache
of an empty stomach.

Lord Jesus:
when
(like James and John)
we want to be at your side
in glory,

remind us where you sit.

Thom M Shuman

MARTHA'S MEDITATION

I never had much time to sit and listen.
Busy about many things.
He was right about that.
Always on the go.
Doing things.
Baking.
Cleaning.
Sewing.
Being useful.

It was what I liked about Him when first we met.
The things He did.
That little girl. Dreadfully ill.
Some even said she died.
He cured her.
I see her with the other children playing at the well.
Her mother never tires of telling the story.

Then there was the time He went crazy in the temple,
turning tables, chasing the moneychangers,
who squawked and bleated as much as the chickens, goats and lambs
running wildly everywhere.
Glorious chaos!
Even now, remembering it I want to laugh out loud.
Hardly orthodox, but He made His point.

Mary has chosen the better part.
That really hurt.
A born dreamer, my sister.
When we were children fetching water or firewood,
she was always mooning over some common pebble or seashell,
saying,
'Look, Martha. Look at the shape. Feel how smooth. See the colours.'
I never understood that really.
Seen one pebble, you've seen them all.
Still she had a knack for arranging the grasses and field poppies
into pretty posies to cheer an ailing neighbour.
Lots of friends, Mary.
People come to talk to her.
A good listener.
When Rachel's baby died it was Mary who sat through

the silences and sobbing; spluttering hurt.
I made myself useful.
Put Rachel's other children to bed and prepared supper for them all.
She was grateful and squeezed my hand in silent recognition.
But there was something in the way she looked at Mary.

The better part!
Doing nothing.
Skiving.
Listening to stories.
And all those questions.
She's always going on about deeper meanings.
Tires me out all that discussion.
Anyway you can't eat words.
No mention of thanks for the bread and soup they'd all scoffed hungrily,
and she, sitting there with them, taking it all for granted.
To tell the truth I don't always understand what Jesus says.
Though there was one story about God being like a woman,
who sweeps her house, looking for a lost coin.
I liked that one
and know the satisfaction of a job well done and a lost thing found.
I always thought that God was too busy to worry about little things
like coins ... like me.
Perhaps I'm the lost coin!
Listen to me –
I'm beginning to sound like Mary.

Anyway the hurtful things He said were forgotten quickly enough.
It was what He did.
He took me by the arm, sat me down beside my sister,
gave us both a conspiratorial smile,
then He turned to my brother.
'Lazarus,' He said, 'help me clear this table.'
And then, rolling up His sleeves,
Jesus did the dishes!

Mary Hanrahan

I USED TO SHOUT

I used to shout a lot,
I had to.
Since I'd been blinded
it was the only way I could get people to notice me.
I couldn't go up to them
so I had to get them to come to me,
so I shouted.

I usually sat on the roadside to beg.
I didn't like begging
but I had no other option.
It's a busy road
between Jerusalem and Tiberias,
lots of people travelling.
I shouted when I heard them coming.
Some ignored me
but others left a coin.
Some stopped a moment to talk with me;
I appreciated that,
begging was often lonely.

One day
the road was very busy.
I shouted out to ask what was going on
and someone told me
that Jesus, the healer from Nazareth, was coming.

I'd heard about him.
They said that he told wonderful stories
and that he could work miracles.
I'd said to myself
that if he ever came down the road
that I would try to get near him,
and ask him if he could heal me.

I knew that I would have to get his attention
so I did what I always did,
I shouted:
'Jesus, Son of David, take pity on me.'

People around me tried to shut me up,
but I kept on shouting.
And he must have heard me.
Someone near me told me to get up:
Jesus was calling me.
People pushed me, bumped against me,
some must have moved back for me.
And then I heard a clear voice in front of me ask me:
'What do you want me to do for you?'
I knew what I wanted and I told him,
'Teacher, I want to see again.'

And he told me to go,
that my faith had healed me,
and as he spoke
I could see again.
I could see the people around me
and the sky and the sun
and I could see him
looking at me
smiling.

When he said to me 'Go'
I could have gone anywhere.
I could walk by myself.
I could see where I was going.
I could choose.
And I chose to go with him.

I don't shout any more,
I don't need to.
But I talk and I laugh
and I cry
and I listen.
And I walk down the road
with Jesus and his friends

Ruth Burgess

LOST AND FOUND

(Luke 15:11–32)

A: Narrator and neighbour
B: First daughter
C: Mother
D: Second daughter

A: There was once a woman who had two daughters. One day one of them said:

B: Mum, I really need some money. You said you were saving up till each of us got married. Can I have my share now?

A: They lived in a village. She'd heard about the bright lights in the city and she wanted to break out, be different, have a good time. So the mother went down to the building society, drew out the money and gave it to her daughter, who bought a one-way ticket for the big city.

There was plenty to spend money on: clothes, pubs, clubs – not to mention food and somewhere to stay. But things were more expensive in the city. Before she knew it, her money had run out. She couldn't pay the rent. She could barely afford a cup of tea. She had to sleep rough. She tried to get a job, but her shabby appearance and lack of any proper address didn't help. She was hungry all the time. Once she got a job washing up in a seedy hotel, and was tempted to eat the greasy scraps that were thrown into the bin.

Some of the others who were on the streets turned to prostitution. She sat in the underpass with a bit of cardboard on which she'd scrawled HOMELESS AND HUNGRY and a few people threw her coins. Then she came to her senses.

B: Here I am asking people for charity, when my mum is always giving money to famine relief. She has a job, too. She sometimes even pays for a service wash at the laundrette. She might pay me to clean the house ...

I'm going home. I'll say to my mother, 'Mum, what I did was wrong, don't call me your daughter any more. But give me a job.'

A: So she set off, hitching and walking, all the way home. She was still at the end of the street, when her mother looked out and saw her lost child! Her heart went out to her daughter, and she ran to meet her, hugged and kissed her. The daughter said:

B: Mum, what I did was wrong. Don't act as though nothing had happened. I'm not your little girl any more.

A: But the mother led her indoors, ran a bath, got clean underwear and her best dress out of the wardrobe, and put these ready for her child to wear. She said to one of the neighbours:

C: Take this money and get me an oven-ready turkey ...

B: I'm a vegetarian.

C: Well, a deluxe pizza then, and a bottle of wine – look, my daughter might as well have been dead, and she's come back to life. She's come home. She was lost and we've found her again.

A: Now the older daughter, who was living at home and going to college and working hard, getting good grades ... she was on her way home. She heard the stereo from the end of the street, and saw people running in and out of the house. She thought:

D: Mum's flipped her lid.

A: She grabbed an excited neighbour.

D: What happened?

A: Your sister has come home and your mum's throwing a party because she's back safe and sound.

The older sister was furious. She leaned against the wall and refused to go into the house. Their mother came out and begged her, but she retorted:

D: Didn't you notice me all these years? Don't I matter? I'm the reliable one. I got a Saturday job and gave you something every week. I never disobeyed you. And you never even let me invite my friends round for a party. Now look what happens when she comes home! She's spent all your savings. She's been living it up. She's been doing goodness-knows-what in the city. She's probably caught something really nasty ... and you throw a party ...

C: My love,

A: Said the mother,

C: You are very close to me. I share everything with you. Won't you share this celebration with me? Your sister was dead and she's come back to life. She was lost and now she's found.

Jan Sutch Pickard

SHEEP AND GOATS

(Matthew 25)

Why sheep and goats, Lord?
Sheep are woolly simpletons,
content to follow-my-leader,
even if the leader is a rogue.

Goats are resourceful,
voracious, surefooted,
independent,
not biddable.

God made sheep and goats.
God made me.
If I am more like a goat
whose fault is that?

Once you were bested in argument
by a woman,
so can this she-goat
please get into heaven?

Josie Smith

IF JESUS HAD SAID YES

(John 10:22–30)

From a sermon

In this Gospel reading Jesus is given a direct request by the crowd: 'How long are you going to keep us guessing? If you are the Messiah, tell us plainly!' Yet, in true Jesus-fashion, he doesn't give a straight answer. He says, 'I have told you and you do not believe me. The things I do by my Father's authority show who I am.'

Jesus often answers around the point when asked directly: When Peter asks who he is, he answers: 'Who do others say I am?' So why does he do this? Why avoid the direct request for an answer?

In helping us understand some of Jesus's reasons for this, let us for a moment imagine that in this particular circumstance Jesus had said: 'Yes, I am the Messiah.' What might the reaction of the crowd have been?

Some, as we know, would have feared him and sought to bring him down either as a heretic or as a threat to the status quo, but let's look at some of the other thoughts that might have gone on in people's heads. Some might have thought, *Excellent, we can sit back and relax now, sure of our impending release from the oppression of the Romans.* Others might have thought, *Hmm, so he is the Messiah; then I guess that means I need to accept and do whatever he says – ordained by God and all that*, and so followed him only out of obligation and authority.

Whatever their thoughts, they would have immediately placed upon him their own expectations and assumptions of what being the Messiah meant, and then felt frustrated, upset or betrayed when those expectations were not met. In knowing the facts, they would have stopped asking the questions.

In not having a black-and-white certainty or proof of Jesus's divinity they were forced to keep questioning; and in doing so, to keep listening and watching and searching. In doing so they were able to discover and own a real faith for themselves.

And so it is with us, I believe. The depth, richness and vitality of our faith comes not in the places where we feel certain of our facts and secure in our beliefs. This security, although comforting and important to us in providing a place of rest and a basis from which to begin, is not often the place of growth in our faith.

Rather it is in the mysteries of our faith – the places of no easy answers, the areas of our uncertainty, or where we are actively open to looking for the truth in many viewpoints – that our faith begins to deepen. It is here in the messiness of creating and shaping and struggling and wrestling, that wisdom and faith come alive in a truly integrated way, one that moves beyond the intellect and into our whole being.

Still, those places are not the comfortable places; the people in the story knew that – they wanted the comfort of facts. Yet Jesus challenged them to move from the comfort and into the mystery, where truth moves beyond fact and must be found and owned by each individual.

So let us also accept Jesus's challenge, and learn to live a little more in the mysteries of our faith – to sit with the uncomfortable questions in our faith, whatever they might be, and to let those places become places of transformation in our lives.

Rowena Aberdeen

JESUS, YOU ARE THE WAY

Jesus, help us to hear you speaking to us in other people,
even in those people we don't like;
the ones who irritate us, bore us and get on our nerves.
JESUS, YOU ARE THE WAY.

Jesus, help us to laugh at our silly ideas of self-importance.
May we learn to see you, serve you and respect you in all our sisters and brothers,
especially in those who are deemed to be of 'no value' in a fast-moving
commercial world,
but who are valued and loved very much by the Father.
JESUS, YOU ARE THE WAY.

Jesus, give us the strength to break through our defences and fears
so that your Spirit freely breathes within us and through us.
JESUS, YOU ARE THE WAY.

Fill us with your Spirit.
Take away our fear,
so that we are not afraid to be vulnerable to people who are hurting through rejection
and the isolation of not being listened to, or valued.
JESUS, YOU ARE THE WAY.

And Jesus, when it becomes hard,
let us rest in you and become strong again.
JESUS, YOU ARE THE WAY.

Jesus, vulnerable one, let us pray to become like you.
Help us always to listen to you, and hear you.
JESUS, YOU ARE THE WAY.

June McAllister, Faith and Light Community, Tuam, County Galway

CHRIST'S WAY, OUR CHALLENGE

(John 13)

(Tune: Old 124th)

Son of the Father, glorious in light,
life of the world, before the world began,
now born among us, living out God's plan,
glory unveiled before our human sight,
you come to us, Lord Christ, the living Way.

Fullness of God, before us now you bend,
take up the towel, and humbly wash our feet,
take up the cross, and make your way complete,
call us to see, love full and without end.
You come to us, Lord Christ, the living Way.

Love is the way we meet the life divine,
love, full and free, in Christ, the Son of God,
love, our response, love is our way, our road.
Thus does the life of God our lives entwine.
We come to you, Lord Christ, the living Way.

We come to you, to learn the way of love:
teach us to serve and share, and freely give,
turn us from self, to help let others live.
Serving below, we share the life above.
We walk with you, Lord Christ, the living Way.

So shall our lives re-echo with your praise,
for in our hearts, however poor and bare,
love, bending low, will find an entrance there.
Come to us, Lord, transforming all our days,
be in us, now, Lord Christ, the living Way.

Leith Fisher

THE PLACE OF HONOUR

A monologue

(Luke 14:7–11)

My master's giving a dinner party for twenty guests this evening.
He often does that, lays on sumptuous meals –
but then he has to, as he gets invited out a lot too!
You know, if I were going to all the trouble and expense
of putting on a banquet,
I'd invite people I really wanted to be there,
people who were good friends.

But not him!
He invites those he thinks he ought to invite –
business people, rabbis, important people –
people he thinks will help him climb the social ladder,
people he hopes will invite him back to their dinner parties
where he can look important!

Although it didn't quite work out like that the other week.
My master was invited to the home of Rabbi Samuel.
He was chuffed to bits when he got the invitation,
strutted about the house like a bird showing off his feathers.
You see, Rabbi Samuel really is an important person in this town –
everyone's desperate to be seen at one of his dos.

So, the day came for this meal, and off my master went.
I went too –
that often happens when there's a big party in the neighbourhood, servants from
other households get dragged in to help out.
So I was there.
I saw what happened.

Well, my master arrived, had his feet washed at the door,
and was shown into the beautifully decorated dining hall –
and it was beautiful!
No expense spared –
cloths threaded with gold, all the best plates, and a feast to behold.
So what does my master go and do?
Only find himself a place right by the head of the table,
as near to the Rabbi as possible.

All seemed to be going well ... until ...
another guest arrived and was shown in.
I knew who this guest was straight away –
he was the Chief Priest of the Temple,
and a good friend of the Rabbi.

My poor master.
It was so embarrassing.
He was asked to give up his seat so that the Priest could be given a place, with his family, near his friend the host.
By then of course several other places at the table had already been taken, and my master found himself
sitting about as far away from the Rabbi as was possible.

And as everyone's heads were turned to the Rabbi,
no one seemed to notice my master was even there!

Kareen Lowther

CLEANSING THE TEMPLE

That's the stuff, Lord!
Let 'em have it, hot and strong.
We've been needing this for a long time,
so clear the lot out!
They're just a lot of hypocrites,
doing very nicely out of 'religion',
yet they don't really
believe a word of it!

But,
why are You looking at me like that?

Ian Cowie

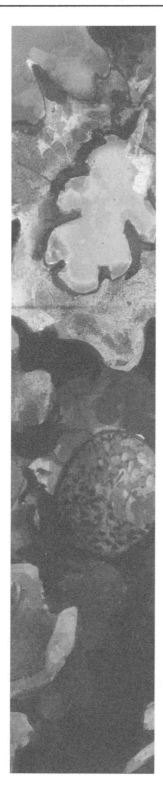

COMMITTED TO THE JUMP
(Luke 11:9)

From a sermon

In this Bible reading, we hear Jesus teaching the disciples to pray and reassuring them of God's active and loving presence in their lives:

Ask, and it will be given you; search, and you will find; knock, and the door will be opened to you. For everyone who asks receives, and everyone who searches finds, and for everyone who knocks, the door will be opened.

Reassuring words it seems, until we look a little closer and see that Jesus, while reassuring the disciples, is also reminding them that this relationship with God, like any other, is a two-way street. We need to ask to receive, search to find, knock before the door opens.

Now this might seem simple enough, but we need to remember here that Jesus was talking to his closest disciples, not a crowd of unbelievers. These were people already committed to Jesus; they had left family and jobs to follow him – why did they need to be reminded to ask, seek and knock – wasn't their commitment already enough?

Perhaps Jesus knew that the disciples, like all of us, even in belief had doubts; we find it hard to hold on to the certainty of God's presence in our lives. We walk a daily journey of having to remember to trust God.

As I was thinking about this passage I was reminded of an activity I used to run at school camps. It involved people being harnessed up to a safety line and then climbing up a 10-metre-high telegraph pole to a tiny one-foot-square platform, which they had to stand up on. About 2.5 metres out and up was a trapeze bar, and the challenge was to jump from the platform and to catch on to the trapeze. Now, this might sound impossible, but the distance was not actually that much more than an outstretched body and arms, easily achievable for most people – the catch lay in that it was only possible to reach if a person committed themselves fully to the jump.

It was interesting to watch people in that situation. A small minority of people committed themselves fully to the jump and of those who did all reached the bar and it was rare for them not to catch it. Even fewer, if any, didn't attempt the jump at all, and climbed back down the ladder. The majority of people did jump, but either with their complete focus on the drop or with last-minute hesitation, both leading to a swing down on the rope and no chance of reaching the bar; they jumped with no belief in their success, no real passion and commitment to their aim.

Sometimes I think we all go about our faith like that last group, at least I see some of that in myself: I believe in the theory; I'm committed to giving it a go of sorts, to getting up the ladder and jumping, so to speak. But still, when it comes down to it, I'm scared of committing myself fully in case my hopes are dashed, afraid that God isn't actually listening or isn't really going to be active in my life, along with all the other fears I hold. This stops me from really going for it and so I just go through the motions half-heartedly or with hesitation and no real faith, and not surprisingly I am a bit disappointed with the outcome. God doesn't appear to hold up his end of the bargain; but in reality I haven't really asked, or knocked or sought; I've pretended to and hoped God wouldn't notice the difference. But the good thing is that God doesn't place the bar close enough for me to remain living in my fears. I grow through finding that courage, and trusting in myself and God, and acting on it in just the same way that those people who commit and leap off the pole and catch that bar glow with the sense of achievement, of conquering their fears, of knowing it is possible and that the bar is solid.

So I think what Jesus was saying here was reassuring – 'Yes, God is there, God listens, God is committed to this relationship with you' – but also reminds us not to forget our side of the relationship – we too have to commit, to trust, to throw ourselves in 100 percent with every chance of looking foolish to the world. If we don't open up the space and opportunities for God to be active in our lives, really open them up, then God has no room to move – no room to be present and respond in any way outside of our limited preconceptions.

God challenges us to be courageous – it reminds me of a favourite quote of mine: 'Leap and the net will appear'*. It underlines our need to trust first, before we know the outcome, before things are certain. Yet God is faithful – our trust will be rewarded, we will be answered, the door will open, the net will be there.

Rowena Aberdeen

* *Zen saying*

LISTEN, PEOPLE OF GOD

Listen, people of God:
The Lord your God is one:
You shall love the Lord with all your heart
and with all your soul and your mind.
You shall love the Lord with all your strength
and your neighbour as yourself.
Listen, people of God.
Listen, people of God.

Carol Dixon

A ROLE MODEL

When I was in my first year of college, I met the person who would have the most profound influence on my life. A friend invited me to go with him to hear the new minister who had just arrived at the church attended by some of the faculty of the college.

Robert had come to this church because he had been 'run off' by his previous congregation in Alabama. Why? Because he believed the promise that the Lord's table was open to all who came from north and south and from east and west, and so had borne witness to this truth by serving the bread and the cup to a black couple, whom the elders of the church had ignored while serving everyone else in the church.

In his new call, he continued to live out this witness. Before it was made law, he taught and lived inclusion, always welcoming whoever came to the door, whether it was at church or at home. He preached justice to a time and a society which was desperately holding on to all its unjust ways. Robert spoke gently the hard words which needed truthfully to be told, he endured the accusations of the critics who charged him with 'meddling', and he provided sensitive and compassionate care to those who spoke vitriolically about him.

For the longest time, I could not figure out why, or how, he did it.

Then one day, when I was visiting him at the church, I needed to use the phone in his office. He waved me behind his desk and left the room to give me privacy. While the phone rang and I waited for the other party to pick up at their end, I glanced down at his desk. There, in a spot where he would see it every day, in the midst of whatever he was doing, was a yellowed piece of paper taped to the desk which simply reminded him in every moment, 'You are a servant.'

Thom M Shuman

HE WAS A STORYTELLER

He was a storyteller,
he drew pictures with words:
a tiny seed growing into a huge tree
a lamp under a bed
a lost sheep crying.
Buckets of fish
hungry birds gobbling up corn
a house built on a rock
workmen grumbling ...

He was a storyteller,
and he told great stories:
Once there was a traveller ... and the bandits attacked him ...
One day a king threw a great banquet ... and no one turned up ...
In a certain town there was a judge ... and there was also a widow ...
There was this man ... and he had two sons ... and they were very different ...

He was a storyteller,
and he asked his listeners questions:
Who was neighbour to this man?
Why do you call me good?
What do you think the owner of the vineyard would do?
Are you jealous because God is generous?

He was a storyteller,
and he knew how to deliver punchlines that stuck in your memory:
No servant can be the slave of two masters.
Whatever is hidden will be brought out into the open.
Whatever you do for the least of my brothers and sisters, you do for me.
Your heart will always be where your riches are.

He was a storyteller,
with words he could draw pictures;
and people listened
and people remembered
and some of them followed him.

They called him
the Word of God.

Ruth Burgess

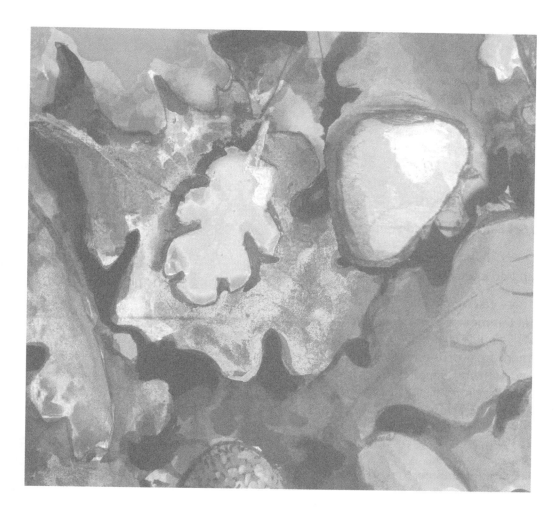

LETTERS

THE JOB

(Acts 12)

I'm not oversure
why I got the job,
but I think
it's because
I enjoy a challenge.

It was sealed orders.

I opened them at midnight.

I read, 'Bust this man out of prison,
and do it tonight.'

There was more:
'At this moment he is asleep in a cell between two guards.
He's double chained.
There are guards on duty inside the prison
and at the prison gates.
Take him into the city
and get him close to
the house of his friends ...
See map below.'

I hadn't much time,
but I had a few minutes to
think of a plan.
Chains and gates
were no problem for me
and I could easily
get past guards,
but I had to take a man with me
and I had no means
of making him invisible.
It was tricky.

Probably best
to get in and out
in a hurry.
I had surprise on my side.

Neither the man nor the guards
knew I was coming.

I took a deep breath and materialised
inside the man's cell.
It was dark
so I made some light.
I shook the man gently,
and as he opened his eyes
I put my finger on his lips
to silence him.
As he stood up
I broke his chains
and got him to dress quickly.
I beckoned him
and he walked
in my footsteps
past the guard posts
and towards the main gate.

He looked dazed,
but I knew he trusted me.

I was wondering
how to tackle the huge gates into the city,
when they swung silently open in front of us.
Someone was monitoring my work that night.
I was glad
and I smiled.

After consulting the map,
I led the man
to a street near his friends' home.
He still looked puzzled.
I think he thought that he was dreaming.
He was safe there.
I could leave him,
mission accomplished.

At a later debriefing

I was congratulated on a job well done
and I was told his name.
He was a disciple of Jesus,
he was called Peter.

I'm resting now,
and wondering what my next job will be.
Whatever it is I'll be up for it.

I'm an angel who loves a challenge.

Ruth Burgess

PAUL HUGGED ME
(Acts 20:7–12)

Last night
Paul hugged me.

I'd gone to hear him speak
and to break bread with the believers.
He'd been in Troas all week
and this was his last night with us.
He still had lots of things
he wanted to tell us.

I'd got myself comfy on the windowsill;
when Paul starts speaking
he can go on for hours.
Around ten o'clock
I could feel myself getting sleepy.
By midnight I could
keep awake no longer.

I woke up in Paul's arms!
Was I surprised!
And we were on the ground floor,
and the meeting had been upstairs.
I was only half awake,
I didn't really know what was going on,

but I remember Paul's smile.
He looked deep into my eyes
and then he hugged me.

I must have gone back to sleep.

When I woke up properly mid-morning
they told me what had happened to me.
I'd fallen sound asleep while Paul was speaking,
and I'd also fallen from a third floor window!
They'd thought I was dead
until Paul came down to find me.

They told me that after that Paul broke bread
and then he went on speaking 'til sunrise.
He left early this morning.

Now, this could be a story
about the dangers of falling asleep
during long sermons,
but I think it's a story
about the love of friends
and of human frailty.

And the best bit is,
Paul hugged me.

Ruth Burgess

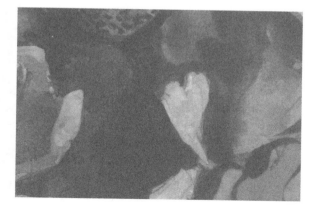

RECOMMENDED DAILY SERVINGS

When that plate of hate
is set before me,
help me to shove it away
and reach for another serving of
love;

when I want to devour
just a handful of despair,
give me a few more morsels of
joy;

tempted to consume
conflict 3 times a day,
entice me with a portion of
peace;

wolfing down agitation
while sitting at my desk,
hand me a bag of
patience;

nibbling
too much on nastiness,
give me a hunger for
kindness;

continually making cold cuts
out of my gifts,
let me spread out a feast of
generosity;

downing a quick breakfast
of oatmeal and apathy,
hand me a bar of
faithfulness
as I dash out the door;

empty the freezer of my heart
of my late-night snacks of vindictiveness,
and thaw it with your
gentleness;

keep me from pigging out
on having things always

(and exactly!) my way,
so I can learn (and practise)
self-control;

these nine servings of fruit
a day
will indeed keep
the doctor of desire
away!

Thom M Shuman

THE FRUIT OF THE SPIRIT
(Galatians 5)

Creator God
we recognise
that we are not as fruitful
as we could be.

Forgive us when we fail
to tend the fruit of the Spirit
and water them with prayer.
FORGIVE US.

Forgive us when we quench
the warmth of love
that enables such fruit to ripen.
FORGIVE US.

Forgive us for those times
when fear causes us
to resist your pruning.
FORGIVE US.

Forgive us when, set in our ways,
we block your growth
in our lives.
FORGIVE US.

Come fertilise our hearts
and bring to fruit in us
your joy and loving kindness.
AMEN

Mary Palmer

AS GOD HAS CALLED YOU

(based on St Paul's letter to the Ephesians)

As God has called you, live up to your calling,
as God has claimed you, live your life in him;
as God has freed you, preserve your freedom,
and come before him full of love and praise.

As God has called you, live your life for others,
as God has loved you, share his love with all;
as God has filled you, live in his Spirit,
and come before him full of hope and faith.

As God has called you, live your life like Jesus,
as God has led you, follow in Christ's way;
proclaim God's kingdom of peace and justice,
and come before him full of joy and grace.

Carol Dixon

DESCENT

(Philippians 2:1–11)

Lord,
You have shown me
Yourself
the way of descent

becoming human flesh
poor and rejected
down
to the utter dereliction
of the cross.

O my Lord
help me to choose
the way of descent
of humility
of taking the lesser part
the lower place

and,
in so choosing,
help me to uncover
the paradox
that the way of descent
leads upwards
to the very heart
of God.

Pat Bennett

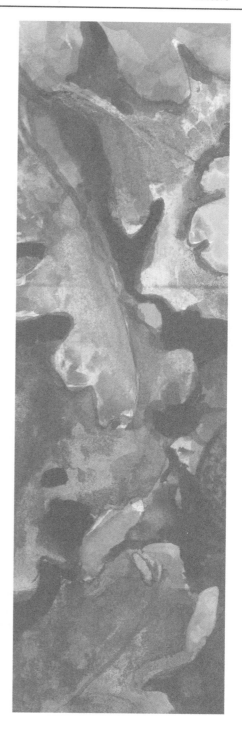

HE EMPTIED HIMSELF

Given in love
before the morning stars
shouting for joy
announced a world was born
                              shorn

O
equality's bright chain!
chosen and sent
to be for our world spent.

Given, exposed
to slander, hate – renounced
parachuting
angel hosts importing aid:
                              made

frail as the least of all,
stands, in our place,
salvation for this race.

Ian M Fraser

A LETTER TO PHIL

Well, I've got a bit of a problem here!
A letter from Paul, that's great!
But who should deliver it but Onesimus!
I never thought I'd see him again.
Onesimus. We used to call him Nessie
(they reckoned he came from Scotland!).
He used to be our slave.
Not a bad worker, could be useful at times
(his name means 'useful' you know).
But, he was useless in the end!
Worse than that,
he stole money from me and ran away.

It seems that he ended up in Rome;
apparently he met up with Paul,
and now he's a Christian!

That Paul, he never gives up!
Well, I owe him.
I also became a Christian because of him.

Now, he's full of praise for me:
I thank God for you,
as an old man, a prisoner ...
(he's under some sort of house arrest, I think).
I received joy and encouragement from your love, etc, etc.
He's leading up to asking a favour!

It seems Onesimus the Christian has been useful to Paul.
He's become like a son to him –
and now he wants me to welcome Onesimus back
as a brother,
a Christian brother!
Welcome him as you would welcome me.
But what about justice?
Nessie stole from me,
he ran away,
he owes me!

What's this?
If he owes you anything, charge it to my account.
But Paul's imprisoned, how can he pay?
Anyway, I'm a respectable businessman;
I'm a church leader too,
we meet in our house,
what will people think?
Nessie's a criminal,
a fugitive from justice.
How can he be my brother?

What did Paul tell us once?
There is neither Jew nor Gentile, slave nor free,
all are one in Christ Jesus.
Well, that's OK in theory,
but in today's world it doesn't work like that,
does it?

What should I do?
What do you think I should do?

David Lemmon

A THESSALONIAN RAP

(1 Thessalonians 5)

A rap for two voices. Words in bold, both voices say together.
Drums might be used.

Listen up, brothers
Listen up, sisters
Listen to the letter
Live out the word

Be at peace, brothers
Be at peace, sisters
Be at peace among yourselves
Be at peace inside yourselves
Be at peace
Be at peace

And we urge you, belovéd
That's you, belovéd
Listen to the letter
Live out the word

Admonish the idlers
Don't let no one be lazy
Encourage the fainthearted
Lend a hand to strugglers
Listen to the letter
Live out the word

Don't hurt each other, brothers
Don't hurt each other, sisters
Don't pay back evil
Seek the good instead

Watch out for everyone
Every child, every grown-up
Watch out for everyone
Lend a hand when your can

And rejoice
Always
Pray
Always

Give thanks
Always
This is what God wants

Do good
Do forgiveness
Do patience
Do encouragement
Do prayer
Do kindness
This is what God wants

Always
Sisters
Always
Brothers
Lister to the letter
Live out the word
Listen to the letter
Live out the word

Ruth Burgess

FAITH WITHOUT WORKS IS DEAD
(James 2:26)

This phrase first gripped me as a teenager trying to make sense of the Christian faith. So many people seemed to believe that faith was about filling pews or going to meetings. Other people seemed to suggest that faith was about what you believed and said.

But I was seeing a God of love and a world in need. And somehow busy churches and right doctrine seemed inadequate, even to miss the point. Faith is not an end in itself. It is the deep-rooted understanding of God's desire for healing and wholeness. It provides the motivation – the compulsion – which drives us outwards to love others and to do all we can to challenge injustice and bring salvation, within God's all-encompassing care.

Thirty years later I am still gripped by this phrase which challenges my complacency and understanding of faith. 'Show me your faith without works, and I, by my works, will show you my faith.' (James 2:18)

Judith Jessop

REVELATION 21 AND 22

John saw a holy city
coming down from heaven,
a beautiful city,
a clean city,
the new Jerusalem.

If you ask me about heaven
I think that I might relocate it;
maybe down to the seaside,
or deep inside a green wood.

Others might fancy an island,
or a journey,
or a village,
or a mountain top covered with snow.

John saw visions and spoke with angels;
some have seen wonders and worked with saints.
I have walked with friends and strangers
and shared love and pain and joy.

Whatever our hope of heaven,
for us
the adventure of death
is still to come,
and we are travelling
home with God.

Ruth Burgess

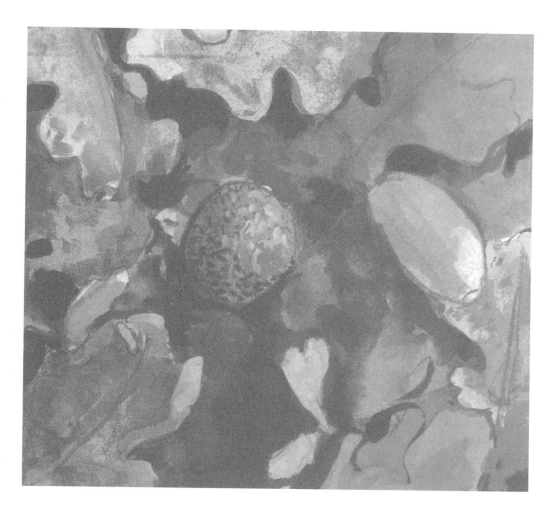

WOMEN'S STORIES

THE CALL

She came to me in the garden;
the sunlight glinting on her hair
a soft chant coming from her lips.
She invited me to follow:
to leave my safe surroundings
to venture to the sea
to board a ship with her
and enter the unknown ...

Julia Brown

WOMEN'S MINISTRY: SOME VOICES FROM THE BIBLE

I am Eve,
half of humanity,
a whole person
in the image of God.
Knowing right from wrong,
I wanted to know more:
I took the apple.
I ate it.
So did Adam.
He blamed me.
I blamed the serpent.
We should have known better.
Is knowledge the problem?
Or disobedience,
or blaming?
I am Eve – only asking.
(*Genesis 1:27; 3:1–24*)

We are Shiprah
and Puah:
wise women,
midwives with attitude.
Who does this man think he is?
Deliver orders, oh yes – but babies?
Our job was never killing children.

How can that be God's work?
So we confused Pharaoh with women's talk,
rolled up our sleeves
and slapped the children of Israel into life.
(Exodus 1:15–21)

I am Miriam.
I danced on the seashore
because the Egyptian soldiers were overwhelmed by the sea.
I led the celebration.
God spoke about history through me.
(Exodus 15:20–21)

I am Mary, God's servant.
A handmaid:
this is hands-on ministry –
and having a baby is just the beginning.
Now my heart cherishes each moment.
In time, it will be broken.
(Luke 1:38; 2:19, 2:41–45; 14:25–26; John 19:25–27)

I am Peter's mother-in-law;
I am not an end-of-the-pier joke.
I was at the end of my tether
when Jesus came to our house,
took my hand, took me in hand,
and suddenly I was myself again.
So I got on with making the meal.
Someone had to do it.
(Mark 1:29–31; Luke 4:38–39)

I am Mary.
And I am Martha.
We welcomed Jesus together
and in different ways:
receiving,
giving,
reflecting,
acting,
listening,
and speaking out,
weeping for the pity of the world,
standing for the truth.

In every human being both of us are at home.
In the story of salvation each of us has a part.
(Luke 10:38–42; John 11:17–41)

I am a mother.
I brought my baby to be blessed.
The busy men wanted to turn me away,
but Jesus told them
I was carrying the Kingdom of God.
(Luke 18:15–17)

I am Joanna, the wife of Chuza.
I know how to run a household resourcefully:
meeting the needs of my family,
and hospitable to strangers.
Now I've gone beyond the boundaries of home,
to provide for Jesus and his friends –
because I can;
because I am also a friend.
(Luke 8:1–3)

I am a Gentile,
an outsider woman
with a sick child.
For her sake I would not be silenced.
I argued with Jesus,
got stroppy,
gave as good as I got.
I was heard.
The child was healed.
(Mark 7:25–30)

I am a Samaritan woman –
I am not a saint.
I gave Jesus a drink of water.
He gave me living water
to revive my spirit and bring me hope.
I told all my neighbours.
They believed because of me.
(John 4:8–30, 39)

We are the Marys.
We stood at the foot of the cross,
and did not avert our eyes from death.
We watched at the tomb.
We came back with spices in the dawn,
met an angel and then –
saw the risen Christ.
We are watchers and witnesses.
(Matthew 27:55, 56; 28:1–10)

I am Priscilla, Aquila's other half.
Our trade is tent-making, so we know
where Paul's coming from;
what's more, we can still make a living when times are hard.
Uprooted from Rome, we settled in Corinth,
made room for a travelling preacher,
and soon there was a congregation meeting in our house.
We both went on mission with Paul.
And when Apollos arrived, and began holding forth,
I make no apology
for taking him in hand
and giving him a good grounding in theology.
(Acts 18:1–3,18,24–26; 1 Corinthians 16:19)

We are the women.
We reminded the men what Jesus taught about his death.
We told them the truth, that Jesus was alive.
They refused to believe us.
What more can we do?
What will it take?
When will they learn?
(Luke 24:1–11)

Jan Sutch Pickard

WHOLLY GOD

If God were a woman
I would be much braver
when it comes
to the heart of the matter;
or rather, when it comes
to matters of the heart.

If God were a woman
I would throw my inhibitions
to the wind.
I would sparkle
and toss and bounce
with laughter and the guts of love
as the sole means of
communication.

If God were a woman
life would be
as light as the topsoil,
as free as the froth, or the frost,
which come and go with the seasons
and the tides and
make a slave of
no one.

If God were a woman
life would be round and full
and tears would conquer fear
which would tremble,
then disappear
in the presence of
such splendid
wholeness.

If God were a woman
life would be complete.
Nothing more. No show.
No great crusade. No mission.
For God would be complete
in you, in me, that's all.

Ruth Harvey

LET MY PEOPLE GO

(Tune: Let my people go)

When Adam was from Eden banned – let my people go!
He blamed it on a female's hand – let my people go!
Go down, Evie, blast high his macho stand,
tell that old patriarch to let my people go!

When Moses said, 'I've done the trick, got God's people out.'
The ghosts of midwives, sisters, mums, raised a mighty shout:
'You did, Moses? Without the likes of us,
guarding your infant life, you'd be down the spout!'

Beyond her time to have a child of the promised line,
Sarah gave her maid to Abe – everything looked fine.
Then came Isaac, quite unexpectedly.
'Humph!' said the patriarch. 'He's yours, but is he mine?'

When Mary had that pregnant look, it was quite a blow,
and raised much doubting in the mind of her faithful Joe.
Said God's angel: 'When God takes things in hand,
kick-starting new advance – men are just de trop.'

The women were not credited when the saviour rose,
their testimony set aside by men deep-sunk in woes.
Good for Jesus! When witnesses where called for,
bypassing all the males, it was them he chose!

Ian M Fraser

FAITH TO FOLLOW (SARAH)

(Genesis 12)

It's OK for you, Abraham,
you're the one who hears the voices,
sees the signs in the night.
But what about me?
I only have your word for it –
that this is the True God.
And now you expect us
to up sticks and set off
for a new land, a new beginning,
at our age; trekking the desert
looking for a new home;
leaving the familiar,
the comfortable for ...
God knows where.
Yet I know your God
is real to you.
Maybe someday
he'll be real to me.
Meanwhile
I'll faithfully follow
in your footsteps
as you follow the Leader,
discovering new hopes,
and new horizons,
every day.

Carol Dixon

THE WOMEN OF THE EXODUS

(Exodus 1:8–2:10; 2:16–22; 15:20–21)

For women working within the system,
ingenuously subverting the establishment,
refusing the tyranny of oppression
with the smiles of feigned innocence:
FOR THOSE WHO ARE MIDWIVES OF THE FUTURE
WE PRAISE THE GOD OF OUR LIBERATION.

For women keeping the tradition alive,
telling their stories and singing their songs,
cradling the future with wisdom
and singing lullabies of hope:
FOR THOSE WHO NURTURE DREAMS OF FREEDOM
WE PRAISE THE GOD OF OUR LIBERATION.

For women exercising leadership and authority,
balancing the ambiguities of status,
risking their hard-won privilege
in alliance with the oppressed:
FOR THOSE WHO SUSTAIN POWER WITH WISDOM
WE PRAISE THE GOD OF OUR LIBERATION.

For women welcoming the stranger,
offering refuge from violence,
providing home and safety
and a place to gather strength:
FOR THOSE WHO SHELTER THE SURVIVORS
WE PRAISE THE GOD OF OUR LIBERATION.

For women who are bold in action,
leading others in new pathways,
taking initiative and disregarding risk
to celebrate the dignity of freedom:
FOR THOSE WHO LEAD OUT THE CAPTIVES
WE PRAISE THE GOD OF OUR LIBERATION.

Jan Berry

GOD, OUR MIDWIFE

(Exodus 1:15–17, 2:1–10)

God, our midwife,
you bring us to birth
accompanying us on our journey.
From our hiddenness
you draw us,
in our hunger
you feed us,
from our bewilderment
you let us go
to proclaim your liberation
through the wilderness
into new ways of becoming.

Elizabeth Baxter

A STORY FROM LONG AGO

Narrator: Long ago, in the days before Israel had a king, three women set out on a long journey ...

Narrator: Day one

Ruth: It was hard to say goodbye to my family, not knowing if I'd ever see them again. My mother cried and my father held me for a long time, and I felt his sadness. I know so little about the land to which I'm travelling. It was hard to walk away from all that is familiar to me, all that has been my home. I'm glad that Orpah, my sister-in-law, is coming with us, because we share the same memories, the same stories. We can help each other along.

Narrator: Day two

Naomi: To be going home was all I ever dreamed of. Ten years in Moab felt like a life-time. I only went there because Elimelech decided that living and working in a foreign land was better than starving in our own village. But Elimelech is dead and both of my sons died in Moab. I am nothing now; a widow without sons has no identity, no protection. My God has deserted me and left me bitter and alone. There was nothing to keep me in Moab, and they say that the harvest will be good this year in Bethlehem. I still have relatives there and I hope that they'll help me. My daughters-in-law, Orpah and Ruth, are coming with me, and I'm going home.

Narrator: Day three

Ruth: Orpah went back to Moab today, back to her home and family. Naomi told her that it made more sense for her to remarry and raise a family in her own community. It was a hard parting. Orpah loved Naomi. We were all in tears. I can't explain why, but I've decided to stay with Naomi. I held on to her and told her that I was going with her. I left her no room for argument. We are travelling on.

Narrator: Day five

Naomi: Why won't Ruth go home? I gave her my blessing. I tried to set her free of any obligation that she feels towards me. I even told her that God has turned against me by taking my husband and sons away from me. But she won't listen. She insists she's coming with me and that nothing I can say will make her change her mind.

Narrator: Day eight

Ruth: I wonder what Naomi's village is like. Will her neighbours remember her? And what will her relatives say when they find out about Elimelech and Mahlon and Chilion? What kind of reception will we get? Will they welcome Naomi, or will they resent her for leaving the village when they were all struggling for survival, for getting out with her husband and sons and leaving the weakest behind? And what will they make of me, with my foreign ways and accent? Will they blame me for what has happened? I'm not someone who was chosen by the God who they believe looks after them, and Naomi thinks her God is punishing her. Will he punish me too? I've said her God will be my God, but I don't know what he's like, this God of hers, or what he demands.

Narrator: Day nine

Naomi: Ruth is still with me. Although her presence is a continual reminder of what I've lost, I'm not sorry. It's good to have a daughter-in-law who loves me like a daughter, like a friend. I'm trying to tell her about my village, my people, about our faith and traditions. But it's so strange to her. And how can I tell her that our God is generous and faithful, when all I feel is bitterness towards him because he has taken from me all that I lived for and loved?

Narrator: Day twelve

Ruth: Naomi says we're getting nearer to Bethlehem. Part of me is excited and part of me is scared. This journey has given me time to think, time to ask questions. I don't feel like the person that I was when we left Moab. I've had to leave behind the things that I don't need any more, to let them go. And I've discovered some of the things that I want for myself, what I hope for, what I dream about, what I need. I can't forget Chilion, or Moab, or my family. I don't want to, they're still part of me, part of the story of who I am. And I know better who I am now. I am Ruth. I am a widow. I am strong. I am able to take risks and to make changes. I am travelling with a new God. Naomi says he looks after his people, fights for them, shelters them, feeds them. He sounds a bit more like a she to me. I'll tell Naomi that one day.

I wish I could share some of this with Naomi. She's so sad at the moment. I want her to know how much I love her, that I want to stay close to her, that I want us to share whatever happens to us from now on.

Narrator: Day fifteen

Naomi: Home is a good place to be and today was both sad and wonderful: wonderful to see my friends and neighbours and catch up on ten years of news and gossip; sad to tell my story, to come home without my husband and sons. It's hard, and yet it feels somehow safe to be back with people who still believe that God loves them and cares for them. Maybe here I can learn to live with my sadness and pain.

This is my home and Ruth is the stranger here, but it's strange for me too. This place is both an ending and a new beginning for me, for both of us. Maybe out of our struggle and suffering something new will be born.

Narrator: And so Naomi returned from Moab, and Ruth the Moabitess, her daughter-in-law, came with her. And as they came to Bethlehem, the barley was ripening and it was harvest time.

Ruth Burgess

JEREMIAH AND THE QUEEN OF HEAVEN

Do you not see what they are doing in the towns of Judah and in the streets of Jerusalem? The children gather wood, the fathers light the fire, and the women knead the dough and make cakes of bread for the Queen of Heaven.
Jeremiah 7:17–18

I don't understand what's going on, why this man rails at us. I don't understand why we shouldn't worship the Queen of Heaven with our date-palm bread as we always have. I don't know why this makes us bad Jews. Does it make all those who've done it before us just as cursed: my grandmother's grandmothers and further back? That I find difficult to believe.

I ask mother but she shrugs. 'Jerusalem ideas,' she says. 'But the old ways will always be with us, no matter what the Jerusalem men think.'

The man is fuming and I'm scared of him. He seems to hate us. He shouts at my father, who is setting off for the fields. Father looks broken. What with famine and nearly losing the land this harvest, he is hardly strong enough to lift his scythe, never mind argue with this full-of-fire man.

My father knows the Queen has saved us in so many ways. Not just by saving our land from the debtors after two years of famine, but by bringing us together. When we celebrate the feast those who have nothing, as we did for so long, can eat the sweet date-palm bread. And then, when we have something, we can give back to those who helped us. Even the wanderers come and sit with us, searching out wood and helping with the fires. How can it be bad?

'How can it be bad?' I ask the man. Is he going to strike me dead? He doesn't. He just looks at me.

'"You shall have one God! says the Lord",' he shouts. Some spit comes out.

I have heard this, but I am not sure why it is important.

'If our God is a Queen God, why can't Abraham be our Father too?' I say.

I think he is going to burst.

'I mean –' I say, getting flustered, 'I mean, does God have to be a man? Creating and healing is woman's work, but God does it.'

I start to back off. His eyes look as if they might shoot fire at me.

He walks off into the hills still shouting. I should have told him the story mother tells when we are together, of how the Queen is God's breath, flowing out from God and making everything alive; how she is a bird flying round us and living with us; how she visits us in our dance and cares for us in our famine.

I would like to tell him more, but he scares me and I have work to do.

Alison Gray

A TALE OF THE GREAT FISH
– a very moral story

A great fish, that's what I am – not one of my smaller cousins, though you'll find plenty of them dotted around the Bible, all doing God's work: fetching temple tax for Jesus, distressing demons for Tobias, imparting wisdom to Job.

No. I am not one of those little tiddlers. I am one of the great fish created by God way back at the beginning of the creation, created even before the land creatures, created well before God dreamed up human beings. Us great fish go back a long way.

And what are we like? Well, Job got the general idea, and a few particulars that he could have done without, when God described us to him. Tails stiff as cedars, bones like bronze tubes, sneezes that radiate light, eyes that glow like the rising sun, the ability to churn up the sea like boiling water and make it bubble like a pot of oil. Us great fish are quite something.

And why did God make us? Well, the psalmist got that right. God made us so that he had beings to play with. God enjoys a good laugh and a rough and tumble. And God's laughter, you know, is infectious, and we are very ticklish, and so is God, but I won't tell you where!

Anyway, enough of the introduction to the story, the story where I am often referred to as a whale. I hope, by now, that you have got the message that I am not. If you haven't, you've not been properly listening.

The time this story happened, I was summering in the Mediterranean. I love the Med; so warm, so cosy. It's a bit of a struggle to squeeze through the Straits of Gibraltar, but it's worth it when you're in. So there I was, dozing on the bottom, when God had a word in my ear.

'The weather,' said God, 'is about to change, and I've got a job for you, so keep listening. I want you to look after one of my prophets for a while, mother him a bit. And give him a safe space to do some thinking and listening. He's got it into his head that he's running away from me. Foolish man – when will he realise that that's impossible? I can be everywhere and anywhere. I want him to do an errand for me, but he's not ready for it yet, he needs to cool his heels for a while, he's a bit of a hothead.

'So,' said God, 'here's what we're going to do. I need a bit of a stormy sea. This prophet, he's called Jonah by the way, is on a boat at the moment. I want to get him thrown off the boat and into the water and to sink down to the seabed. And when he thinks he's had it, I want you to swallow him and hang on to him for a few days and I'll sort things out after that.'

'He'll be scared,' I said, 'scared of drowning – and even more scared of me.'

'That's all right,' said God. 'He'll cope. With people like him I have to scare them a bit before they'll listen to me.'

'Anyway,' said God, 'the storm: If you and I have a game of leapfrog up top with a few spectacular splashes, and I throw in the odd thunderbolt or two, that should do the trick. Are you ready?'

'Definitely,' I said.

And so it happened – a storm, man overboard, down to the bottom of the sea, and gulp. Poor Jonah, it was worse than his nightmares. However, at this point I'd better correct any false versions you've heard of this story. A lot of people think that being inside me was the worst thing that happened to Jonah. Wrong. If they go back and read the story they'll find that Jonah's bad time, the seaweed round his neck, the panic, etc, all happened before I got to him. I was the one who saved him!

I had three days of Jonah's company. I can't say I really noticed him much. He was no weight at all. I don't know what God said to him, but I suspect that he listened, after all he can't have had too many distractions. Though it must have been a bit bumpy for him – especially when God and I played ring-a-ring o' roses around the Greek Islands.

At the end of three days God must have thought that Jonah was ready to do as he was told, and told me to swim towards the shore; and then she tickled me, and I rolled around near the shore, had a bit of a cough and Jonah landed up on the beach.

He looked a bit sticky, and very bemused, but God must have told him to get going, because he never looked back. Apart from a rumour of him talking to a castor oil plant, I never heard of Jonah again.

And so to the moral of the story:

First, remember us great fishes. We are not whales. We do not all live in Scottish lochs. And God enjoys our company, and we hers.

Secondly, we are wise and we are good storytellers. Listen to us sometimes and see things from our viewpoint. We've seen a lot of history in our time.

Thirdly, and lastly, I must remember what I learnt from my encounter with Jonah. I'll need to watch my diet. Some people, they make me sick!

Ruth Burgess

MARY MAGDALENE – A REFLECTION

(Luke 7:36–50; Luke 8:1–12)

So who was this woman, this sinner,
who did such a memorable
and extravagant
and loving thing?
Was this woman the same
as Mary Magdalene 'from whom
seven demons had gone out'?

Would we recognise her
if she walked into the room
or sat down beside us,
or reached out to touch us?
Would we recognise Mary,
with or without her seven demons?

And what were they like,
those seven demons?
Those afflictions, ailments, imperfections,
those accidents of birth,
those distracting facts of life,
that obsessed her, possessed her,
and defined her in everyone's eyes?
What form did they take?
Would we recognise them
if they crossed our path
or entered our lives?

One: Breaking the rules,
crossing social boundaries,
defying religious laws!

Jesus would recognise that – he did those things too.

Two: Selling her body!
Did she have a choice?
What do we know
about the economics of her situation?
Her story?

Three: Enjoying sex!
What? Surely not!
The demon might lie in enduring it –

not entering freely
into a loving physical relationship,
but being dragged down
by power games and loathing.

Four: Breaching the peace;
being a cause of alarm and distress,
shock and scandal!

We can't have that –
though some folk enjoy scandal more than sex.

Five: Being lost for words:
struck dumb by guilt!

Who had ever cared what she said?
Or maybe she was silenced
by something that happened to her.
But she learned that actions speak louder than words.

Six: Being different
Enough said.

Seven: Low self-worth!
'I'm rubbish,' she used to say.

Not believing in her value as a child of God,
denying the spirit of God at work in her.

Seven demons

But Jesus saw the woman,
saw God at work in her,
as she welcomed him,
cared for him, dared to touch him:
Jesus recognised the generosity
with which she anointed him
and knew the grace that let her tears flow freely.

They called her a sinner.

But Jesus called her a loving woman:
Forgiven, faithful, saved.
'Go in peace,' he said.
But she chose to follow him.

Jan Sutch Pickard

FOR THE WOMAN WHO DARED TO ANOINT JESUS

Good girls don't drink,
good girls don't swear,
good girls don't think about sex,
good girls don't think about themselves,
good girls aren't pushy,
good girls don't get angry,
good girls don't have passion,
and they certainly don't scream or shout.

This girl does.

A good enough girl.

Good enough to love Jesus,
good enough to be loved by Jesus.
Good enough to serve Jesus,
good enough to serve for Jesus.
Good enough to talk to Jesus,
good enough to talk for Jesus.
With love.
With joy.
With anger.
And with passion.

What do you say now?

Karen Jobson

A WOMAN'S PRAYER

Lord Jesus, you know how life goes.

Pain of childbirth, hoping for safe delivery,
and pain of barrenness, longing to love.
Lord Jesus, be with us.

Hardship and economic suffering,
anxiety about a partner's job, or earnings
to cover school fees, books and uniforms.
Lord Jesus, support us.

Old age of parents and loved ones, caring,
confusion as death encroaches on our lives,
inability to protect even our young ones from sickness and death.
Lord Jesus, enfold us.

We long for our children to succeed, to fly,
yet this pierces our heart for a while,
but secretly we feel a certain pride.
Lord Jesus, encourage us.

Yes, Lord Jesus, you know how life goes.
You are a man, more gracious, kind and understanding,
than all men put together.
Lord Jesus, thank you.

Francine E Asonibare

BECAUSE SHE CARES

Each day
God the Mother walks with me.

She holds my hand
at busy crossroads,
reminds me to be careful
because it matters to her
what happens to me.

She points out rainbows
when my mind is busy
on the deluge of paperwork
impatient on my desk.

She smiles at me
from the newsagent's eyes,
and with a blackbird's song.

God the Mother walks with me
and my heart skips along.

Nancy Somerville

REMEMBERING THE WOMEN

God who shows us a father's and a mother's love,
we give thanks for women who have shown your love.

We remember and name before you now:

those women who, in their stories and prayers,
have nurtured our faith ...

those women who offer simple hospitality
and welcome to the stranger ...

those women who work to build bridges in communities ...

those women who, at some risk to themselves,
live out their faith in the hard places of this world ...

We celebrate these grandmothers, mothers and sisters in Christ,
in whose lives your love is revealed.
May their labours not be in vain,
and may we be counted in their number –
faithful followers of Christ,
building community,
working for the Kingdom.

Alison Adam

Note: Names may be spoken in the silences and then 'gathered up' in a chant such as 'Lord, draw near', or 'Ubi caritas'.

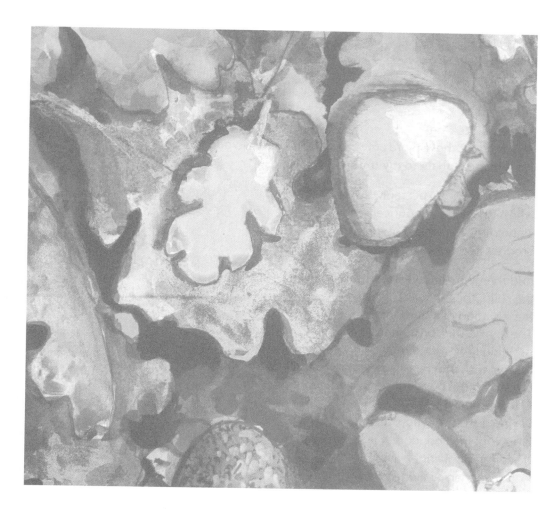

SAINTS

A PROTESTANT REFLECTS ON THE FEAST OF THE ASSUMPTION OF THE BLESSED VIRGIN MARY

'Queen of Heaven'
Why is it that those words of favour, reverence, devotion,
seem inappropriate to my untuned ear?

Mary, visited unexpectedly by God's angel,
whose shocking announcement –
'Behold the handmaid of the Lord' –
brought her trembling acceptance.

And then the silent years of motherhood,
the child, the homelessness,
the devotion of a husband.
The family, the constant little efforts of providing,
growing food, grinding, baking, talking, sharing.
Always with others, village women and children,
but watching, pondering, musing, remembering
God's promise.
Seeing Jesus growing, smiling,
laughing, making, doing, learning, leading,
deciding, resolving, leaving.
And then, herself alone grieving,
hearing, puzzling, wondering, fearing,
resisting, struggling, accepting,
following to Jerusalem.

'A sword piercing my heart'.
Yes, on that day, nails in my hands and feet too.
I would not have it otherwise.

High King of heaven, I worship thee,
and that is all the joy for me.
Privilege enough your mother to have been,
I would they did not call me queen.

And so she lifts her heart in praise.

Liz Gregory-Smith

ADOMNÁN REFLECTS

Adomnán was Abbot of Iona from 679–704. 'Adomnán's Law' prohibited the killing or enslavement of women and children in war.

There will, of course, always be wars and rumours of wars;
rulers will persuade their people that they have just cause
to invade their neighbours or folk in far-off land
and that such conflict is glorious, great and grand,
but now at least it is written as a law
that the innocent should not suffer in a war.
Women and children should not be used
as slaves or hostages or in other ways abused.
We have had the courage to decree that it is wrong
for the weak and helpless to be bullied by the strong.
A monk I may be but I am not naive,
I know that men who use lofty words to state what they believe
may still commit atrocities and abominations,
but now they know that this is sin and will receive just condemnation.
And so in the great work that Christ has begun
I have played my small part; that at least I have done.

Brian Ford

PRAYER FOR ST FRANCIS DAY

(October 4)

God of unrelenting beauty,
you are the origin and home of our deepest longing;
you are the beckoning word
that draws us into the truth of ourselves.

Through Jesus Christ,
through the Holy Spirit
and through one another,
may we be released
from all that stands in the way of real freedom,
so that,
naked to the eyes of the world,
we may revel in the rich garments of your grace and truth. Amen

Julie Greenan

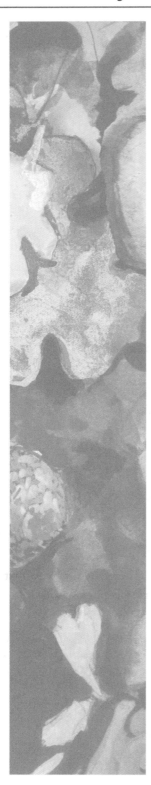

THE JESTER'S ANTHEM

St Francis of Assisi called himself 'God's jester'.

I'd rather be a jester than a king
and play midwife to chuckles and guffaws,
for laughter is a very precious thing
and making it's as fine as making laws.

And when the crowned heads roll as roll they must,
new faces and new dogmas take command
and once-proud sacred cows lie in the dust,
the jester's craft will still be in demand.

And he who scorns the jester's humble play
is a joyless, brain-dead, soulless sort of clod.
For laughter is one step upon the way
that brings us closer to the throne of God.

Brian Ford

PRAISE
(after St Francis)

Composer of the cosmos
all offers you praise:

Brother Sun
who orchestrates our days

Sister Moon
singer of light and tides

Brother Wind
who gives voice to the skies

Sister Water
her music fluent through streams

Mother Earth
who nurtures each season's song.

May we too share
your bounty.

Mover of mountains
enable us to change.

Mary Palmer

A SIMPLE ACT OF COURAGE

When I was growing up in Alabama, her name was spoken with the same kind of contempt and hatred one would use when uttering a profanity.

For some, it was because she was a woman who did not know her place. For others, it was because she was a black person who did not know her place. For many, it was because she was the one who had 'started' all the trouble that plagued the state and the nation. And for just about everyone around me, it was because of all three that her name was anathema.

We'll never really know if her feet hurt so much that she couldn't take another step. But we can be certain that her soul ached from years of the pain of people looking down on her because of the colour of her skin.

She may not have been so physically tired that she couldn't lift herself from that seat in the front of the bus. But there is no doubt that her heart was weary from all the names she had been called since she was born.

While she could have simply acquiesced to the request to give her seat to a white man, she simply refused to move … causing a seismic shift in America by her simple act of courage.

This past weekend, the body of Rosa Parks was viewed by thousands in Montgomery, Alabama, where the civil rights movement began. The descendants of her spirit, black and white, came to honour her courage, her character, her witness.

For this former 'cuss word' is now the byword for justice, for hope, for action throughout the world.

And today, her body lies in the rotunda of the nation's Capitol Building, the first woman to be so honoured, because she honoured us with her grace, her wisdom, her gentleness.

How appropriate that yesterday's Gospel reading contained these words: 'The greatest among you will be your servant. All who exalt themselves will be humbled, and all who humble themselves will be exalted.' (Matthew 23:11–12)

Thom M Shuman

FOR SAINTS' DAYS

We join hands
with the living
who are learning to love.

We dance
with the dead
whose vision still lives.

We pause
with the angels
in remembrance.

Elizabeth Baxter

PRAYER FOR ALL SAINTS' SUNDAY

God of surprises,
give us humility
that we may receive from those who think they have nothing to give;

wake us up and keep us alert
to recognise your face in the last place we expect;
draw us into the gathering of your saints,
all those who are Christ's friends. Amen

Julie Greenan

IN THESE ISLES

Once
in these isles
a young woman,
who had recently
arrived in a country,
went to the king of that country
and asked for some land,
on which to build a nunnery.

The king, who had no intention of parting
with one square inch of his land,
smiled.
'I will give you,' he said,
'all my land on which
snow falls tonight,'
and he sent the woman away.

The king's advisers were impressed.
The king had not refused the woman
but neither was he likely to lose any land.
It was, after all, a bright midsummer's day.

The young woman
returned to the cave where she was sheltering
and prayed.

That night, it snowed.

The king, who was a just king, laughed.
He knew when he was beaten.

Bega got her land
and settled down in Cumbria,
and she cared for her neighbours,
and prayed for the king.

Next time the weather amazes you
remember Saint Bega
and the God of surprises,
and a summer's night
full of snow.

Ruth Burgess

THE THIRTY-FIRST DAY*

I remember those who have died:
those who were part of my living
those who live on in my life.

God of the elements, You inhabit me:
family and friends and strangers are at home in me,
stars and planets dance in my bones and blood.

I am me,
and yet I am more than me;
I remember, I learn, I dream,
I touch death and life.

God of eternity,
comfort your people,
living and dying.

Quicken us with wonder,
salt us with justice and integrity,
welcome us with love.

Ruth Burgess

*On the 31st day of the month, the Iona Community remembers
and prays for members who have died and their families.*

ANGELS

NO SHOES

An angel is a little thing that flies
and wears no shoes.
Sometimes it is invisible
but all the time it goes about
doing good things
and making people happy.
Oh yes and it also has a harp,
then it can sing songs
to help people forget their troubles.
There are some bad angels
who are called fallen angels.
They're probably the ones that
come in the night
and give you nightmares.
I would hate to be a fallen angel
because they don't have wings
and so they just do what they say
and fall all over the place.

Kirsty Thomas, aged 9

First published on a poster to celebrate the installation of 'The Angel of the North',
a sculpture in Gateshead.

ANGELS

Angels.
Angels in Bible stories.
Angels in and out of our lives.

Michael: defeater of dragons, destroyer of evil.
Raphael: matchmaker, healer, traveller.
Gabriel: messenger, teller of truth.

And another name, Lucifer,
the brilliant one, who fell from the heavens,
the son of the morning, the star of the dawn.

Angels.
Angels whose names are not known to us –
making Sarah laugh,
and Jacob limp,
and Balaam tremble;
letting Peter out of prison,
advising Paul.

Questioning angels and challenging angels,
guardian angels who cradle little ones,
angels who see travellers safe home
and safeguard stumbling feet.

Angels.
Angels all around us.
God's confidantes,
God's messengers.

Angels
full of truth
and full of glory,
bright with joy.

Ruth Burgess

AT THE HILL OF THE ANGELS

Lord of the touch –
here I am.
Consecrate my body – head, heart, hands, feet –

that today, by some word or action,
I may be your angel
to touch someone You love.

Pat Bennett

The Hill of the Angels is a stopping place on the Iona pilgrimage.

MICHAEL VISITS THE ABBEY *

Michael gets up and walks out of his home in the wee chapel and comes to join us here in the cathedral. It's rare for us to specifically invite him, but he usually comes anyway; after all, our work is similar in some ways to his.

He removes his helmet, as I do my hat, and then he stoops low to enter the cloister door. His silver sword gleams with light. He looks around, spots an old lady sitting on her own, sits down next to her. The chair is too small for him; the bottom of his wings disappear down into the floor.

He listens to our words. Everything we know is reflected in his silver breastplate: the devastation of our rainforests, ethnic unrest, street children, air miles, poverty. Michael is as at home in our world as he is in the heavens.

When we sit in the cathedral, this ancient house of prayer and peace, Michael and the angels sit with us. Energy sparks, prayers form, creativity crackles. God is here in the miracle of community.

Simon de Voil

* *On Iona, the Michael Chapel is a small building to the north of the Abbey; the Abbey is also known as St Mary's Cathedral.*

IMAGINE

Close your eyes ...

Imagine there's someone behind you or beside you.
They're ready to catch you if you stumble.
They'll save you from falling.

Who do you see?
Do they have wings?
Are they shining brightly?

Maybe your angel is a creature of light.
Maybe your angel is the woman
who smiled at you when you passed her in the street.

Who do you see?
Who are the angels in your life?

Open your eyes and thank God for your angels.

Anikó Schütz

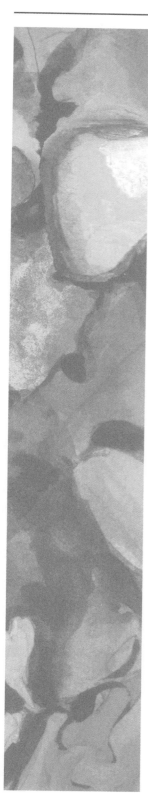

A SORT OF WARNING

Don't mess with God's angels.
I mean it.

Don't play games
or dress up the truth.
Don't tell bad stories.

God's angels move
between earth and heaven.
They are free.
You cannot tame them.

They can lift you up.
They can strike you down.
They will tell you
what God wants you to know.
Make sure you listen.

God's angels
are guardians,
keeping safe your body
holding tight to your soul.
Let them do their job in you.
Don't resist them.

God's angels are holy and strong.
They are beautiful.
So are you.
Don't forget it.

But,
remember,
don't mess with God's angels,
ever.

Ruth Burgess

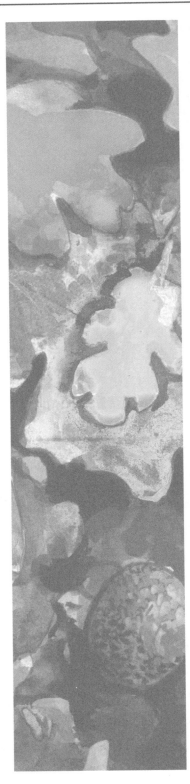

IMAGES

As a child
my father took
me walking in woods
and round reservoirs.
On wet days
we walked in art galleries
and museums.

In one gallery,
at the top of the stairs
was a pedestal,
and on it was
a golden figure,
taller than a human,
with outspread wings.

In Sunday school
I had heard of
'Gentle Jesus'.
I had seen pictures
of him, smiling,
with his arms
around children.

In the gallery
this figure
on the pedestal
felt strong
and powerful.
I was attracted to him.
Perhaps this was
'Almighty God'?

As an adult
I retraced my steps.
The golden figure
was still in
the gallery,
but had been
moved from
the top of the stairs

into the Edwardian
tea room.

Despite
his new surroundings,
he was still strong
and powerful.
He was very beautiful.

I bent to read
the words
I had not read
in childhood:
'Sculptor, Jacob Epstein.
Title, 'The Archangel Lucifer'.

Ruth Burgess

'The Archangel Lucifer' is in Birmingham City Art Gallery. Currently the sculpture is in the gallery shop.

ANGEL IN DISGUISE

I hated him.
He undermined me,
threw daggered words and spiteful looks,

tore me down and tired me out.

He found every weakness,
entered every wound and insecurity.

And in doing so, forced me to look into my own shadows.
Am I truly a person of love and compassion?
Or does it fall away like an inconvenient cloak
when I'm backed into a corner?

I wrestled daily with him
and with my integrity;
like wrestling with Jacob's stranger
an angel in disguise.

Rowena Aberdeen

MY GUARDIAN ANGEL

I have a guardian angel,
and I'm really not quite sure
whether you'll believe me when I tell you so!
I have a guardian angel,
even though I think that you're
still convinced that I went loopy long ago!

I have a guardian angel,
but it matters not a jot
whether you believe it's fantasy or real.
I have a guardian angel,
though you think that it is not
just the kind of thing that really should appeal.

I have a guardian angel,
since the age of nine or ten
she's kept me safe when I was really scared.
I have a guardian angel,
and even bogey men
couldn't harm a child who was so well prepared.

I have a guardian angel,
even though I don't expect
this is something that you'll ever comprehend.
I have a guardian angel,
so, please, show some respect
for my constant guide, my everlasting friend.

Tom Gordon

STONE ANGEL

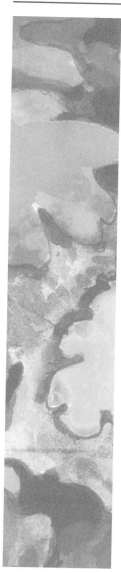

Stone angel
high up
bearing the weight of heavy beams.
Stone angel
high up
breathing the hot air of endless good words.
Stone angel
high up
caught in the steady beam of a spotlight.
Cold, stone-captured, hemmed in and helpless.
Oh that you could spread your wings
and contradict the notion
of security and guardianship
that masons made you long ago
and we have today accepted.
That you could be free to meet us,
comfort us,
challenge us,
even frighten us,
in warm flesh and flashing wings
bringing us clearly the message of God.
Stone angel
high up
symbol of our desire to make safe
the terror and majesty of the living God.
Stone angel
you make me very sad.

Ruth Burgess

I'VE COME TO LIGHT THAT CANDLE

(John 1:5; Ephesians 5:8–11; James 4:7–8)

In horns and a red cloak, the devil stands centre stage as guardian of the candle. The candle should be large and easily seen. A box of matches should be available nearby. Five characters, one after the other, move onto the stage in order to light the candle. They can enter from any direction … but will each one manage to get past the guardian?

First person enters and makes his/her way towards the candle.

Devil: What are you doing here?

First person: It's too dark in here, so I thought I'd light that candle.

Devil: Come off it! You've never been any good at anything, you'd prob-
                  ably knock the candle over – sit down!

First person leaves. The devil laughs and looks pleased and shouts: 'EA-SY (clap, clap, clap). EA-SY (clap, clap, clap).'

Second person enters, and moves towards candle.

Devil: What are you doing here?

Second person: It's a bit dark in here, so I'm going to light that candle.

Devil: You don't have to do it now. Nobody makes important decisions just
                  like that *(snaps his fingers)*. You've got the rest of your life to make up
                  your mind. Go away and think about it, take your time.

Second person leaves. Devil laughs and looks pleased and shouts: 'EA-SY (clap, clap, clap) EA-SY (clap, clap, clap).'

Third person enters, and moves towards candle.

Devil: What are you doing here?

Third person: Well, it's a bit dark in here, so I was just going to light that candle.

Devil: You! You haven't got the time. What with your exams coming up,
                  your homework to do, your computer games, and the sports clubs
                  you go to. In fact you'd better hurry – I thought you were meeting
                  all your friends at eight o'clock! *(If this character is an adult, then sub-
                  stitute these activities for adult commitments, i.e. housework, family,
                  meetings, the gym, etc.)*

Third person leaves. Devil rubs hands together, looks pleased and shouts: 'EA-SY', etc.

Fourth person enters, moves towards candle, picks up the box of matches.

Devil: What do you think you're doing?

Fourth person: It's dark in here, so I thought I'd better light the candle.

Devil: Go ahead! *(pauses while fourth person strikes a match)*. But they'll laugh at you, call you awful names: 'Fanatic', 'Religious Freak', a member of the 'God Squad'. They'll say you're 'Over the top!'. Don't be the first one to make a move, let someone else do it.

Fourth person blows out the match and exits.

Devil looks extremely pleased, laughs loudly and shouts: 'EA-SY', etc.

Fifth person enters, moves towards the candle.

Devil: And what are you doing here?

Fifth person: It's very dark in here, so I've come to light the candle.

Devil: You're too young.

Fifth person: What's that got to do with it?

Devil: You're not intelligent enough.

Fifth person: What's that got to do with it?

Devil: Well, you're not brave enough.

Fifth person: What's that got to do with it?

Devil: *(looking really worried, yells:)* You're not good enough!

Fifth person: That's got nothing to do with it.

Devil: Then why are you so keen to light the candle?

Fifth person: *(lights candle)* Because it's better to light one candle than forever curse the darkness.

Devil shrinks back, covering himself with his cloak, and slinks away …

Sheila Hamil

DANCING WITH ANGELS

Child
you are my burning bush.
Resting my eyes on you I see God
and the angels
swirling
whirling in around you.

Girl
you are my still small voice.
In your gentler pace
in your 'Go slower, Mummy'
I hear the sound of God (and the angels)
listening in the spaces between us.

Babe
your footsteps are my holy ground.
Angels sing from your eyes, your lips,
through your giggle,
in your gently sleeping breath.

In my rushing,
I lose eye contact,
I dance a different dance.
I move too fast.

You are the sacred ground of my being.
Let us touch, skin to skin –
me, stripped naked of my shield of busyness –
let us dance an angel dance together.

Ruth Harvey

ENTERTAINING AN ANGEL?

Three nights ago a brown dove arrived at my dovecote,
a stranger among my white birds.
It was there again the next night,
and the next.
And this morning I caught it helping itself to my corn.
I thought,
A quick grab, a skilled twist:
pigeon pie tonight.
But that would be a cruel betrayal of hospitality.
Shouldn't that verse in Hebrews about entertaining angels unawares
apply to doves?
And humans?

Brian Ford

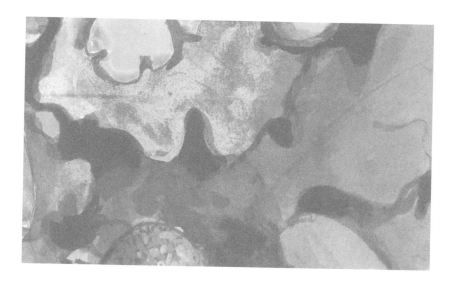

TWO WINGS

An angel
is a bit like a tooth fairy
but it does not collect teeth.
An angel is a good person,
but,
maybe it is not.
An angel has two wings and it wears pink,
but,
it might not.
An angel is a dead person, that's definite.
I think when you are dead you pass a test.
You go down to earth and do good things for the best.
You help somebody in need.
That means doing good deeds.
If you get all the deeds right
then you can be an angel and fly at night.
It's my dream to see a real angel.

Adam Pearson, aged 10

*First published on a poster to celebrate the installation of 'The Angel of the North',
a sculpture in Gateshead.*

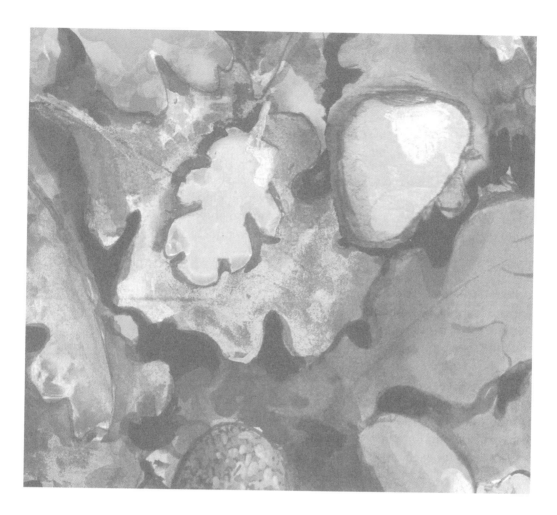

HARVEST

LIFT YOUR HEART

(Tune: Uist tramping song)

Lift your heart, sing for joy, scatter dullness, banish sadness;
lift your heart, sing for joy, welcome goodness, summon gladness.
In the colours of creation, see God's glory, see God's goodness,
and in joy and exaltation, lift your heart, sing for joy.

Blue the sky and blue the sea, ever restless, ever-changing,
sign of Spirit, living, free, o'er our world for ever ranging.
Green of grass and field and forest, fruit of planting and of sowing
show the living God is with us, present in all growing.

Chorus

Gold the sunlight, gold the harvest, warm and ripe and full of food;
eat and laugh and share together and give thanks that God is good.
Red the earth, ground of all growing, red the blood of deeper hue,
red the cross, the cost of knowing of God's love for you.

Chorus

See the colours dance together, dark and bright and pale and strong,
tell the story of the glory of the way we all belong.
For we all belong together – let us share God's gift as one,
and in living for each other, love will ever run.

Chorus

Leith Fisher

A NINETY-THREE-YEAR-OLD WOMAN TALKING ABOUT APPLES

'In ancient times we used to get all types of apples. We used to get Thamey Sweets, St Lawrence, crabs, russets, candy-striped, sheep's nose. Like a sheep's nose, yes. Sort of tapered. My mother would bake Thamey Sweets – and the skin would shine. So sweet you didn't need sugar. You just left the stem on and added cloves. A squatty kind of apple. God – the smell when they're baking,' sighed the old woman, and closed her eyes. Like it suddenly all came back to her. On a wave.

Thank you, God,
for the wisdom of ninety-three-year-old women:

food for thought.

Thank you for apples. For Thamey Sweet apples,
St Lawrence apples, crab apples,
russet apples, candy-striped apples,
sheep's nose apples...

For the precious and amazing
diversity of your world.

May we never take that wealth for granted.
May we work to guard and secure it.
May we be full of wonder.

In the name of the One God:
the one God of many apples.
Amen

Neil Paynter

THE FRUITS OF LOVING

In the joy of conversations,
in the laughter of jokes,
in the risk of encountering personality,
in the fear of exposed vulnerability,
in the danger of loving,
in the unpredictability of all relationships.

In the midst of all of these,
we find strength for the way.
Affirmation of our humanity,
solace for our souls.
We glimpse the deep potentials of life,
the joy of growth, and the realisation of our identity.

For the way of love is at cost,
a way of pain, brutality and risk.
But a way which is of life in all it's fullness.
A life which blossoms with the seed of our human potential.
The life we were meant to lead is found.

Scott Blythe

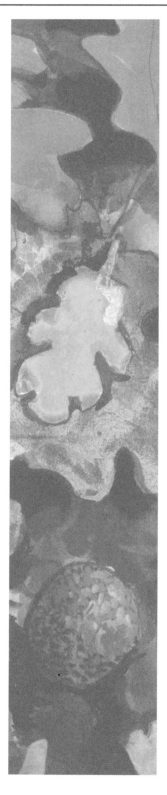

HARVEST

One autumn afternoon,
after the night's storm,
the ground in a country field
was littered
with green shells
and shiny brown conkers.

We arrived,
leaving behind us the traffic and city streets;
Peter, ready to hurl sticks,
Gary, not quite sure if he felt sick and
Glen, silent and thoughtful.

They found it hard to believe;
as we moved from tree to tree,
there were conkers and conkers and
still more conkers;
no need even to shuffle through the leaves
or prise open tight shells –
just reach down and gather them in.

Gary, if Jesus ever told a true parable about you,
it was that of the farmer
who built more and more barns;
having stuffed your pockets,
you proceeded to fill your socks,
'til at last you gave in
and turned to climbing trees.

Glen, not quite believing it all,
asking, tentatively,
if you could keep some for yourself.

Peter, helping me fill the bag,
laughing and picturing Gary
taking home enough conkers to fill his bedroom.

Glen, you made us all laugh
when, on hearing the church bells,
you asked if ice-cream vans
came out this far into the country.

In the car home we talked,

laughing as the wind blew papers
all over the back seat:
Glen describing the beautiful girl he'd marry,
Gary shouting 'Giddy-up' to a passing horse.

And so we returned home;
back to the maisonettes and tower blocks,
having shared in the autumn harvest.

Ruth Burgess

HARVEST WRAPPINGS

God hides his living seeds
in rosy apples, ripening pears
and juicy oranges;
in red tomatoes, rounded swedes
and long, green dangling runner beans.
To hang the trees with purple plums
God sends the sun and rain in bouts,
and vines with luscious grapes are decked
while fields yield broccoli and sprouts.

As harvest-time returns,
the varied ways in which God wraps
life-giving seeds
make for a colourful display
of fruit and flowers of every kind;
beauty of pattern and design.
This is a feast for all to share,
filling our hearts with gratitude
for God's incessant love and care.

So when, in many lands,
we eat the fruit and sow the seeds
in partnership with God,
he feeds us with delicious food,
renewing body, mind and soul,
and blesses us in many ways.
Then we, in glad responsive love,
will give him joyful thanks and praise.

Beryl Chatfield

POPPIES

Scything through the tares,
does the Harvester come across the poppy and stare,
disarmed by its audacious beauty
standing fragile amongst the wheat?

Does he stoop to consider
this lily of the field
alien amongst the uniform rows?

Does he kneel in wonder at its growth
and feel keenly for its strangeness,
and the oddness of its fruit?

Does he lay down his scythe
and smile at the diversity of his creation?
Does he take heart that it manages to exist at all?

For he knows the ground into which it fell,
the seed from which it grew,
the storms it has endured,
and the dark crows that have overshadowed it.

Will he cut it down
or carefully garner it?
Will he burn it
or gently carry it home?
Will he discard it
or add to its number?

In his Father's house are many rooms.
It would not be surprising if
armfuls of poppies
decorate them all.

Lisa Debney

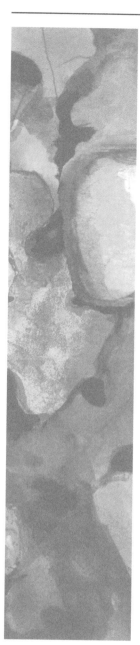

TABLET

(a recipe – by Grace)*

I was making tablet one day,
and I thought it's like this:
the sugar is the sweetness of the Lord;
the milk is the nourishment of his word;
the butter is the oil of salvation.
It's all put into a vessel – which is us –
and warmed by God's love.
Then it has to be laid out, like the life of Christ.
And then, of course, it has to be shared.

*As told to Jan Sutch Pickard by Grace MacDougall

UNDER THE LEMON TREE

For Afaf Shatara in the West Bank

Under the lemon tree
there is a table spread:
a place of hospitality
and breaking bread.

From the garden, ripe fruit:
pomegranate, fig, pear;
round the table, friends meet,
blessed to be there.

Fresh olive oil, soul food,
sweet pastries to share:
O taste and see that God is good;
know that God is here.

Jan Sutch Pickard

GOD OF THE HARVEST

God of the harvest
God of the land
forgive our greed,
our over-building
and mass production,
our wastefulness.
Bless those who work on the land:
farmers
fruiterers
labourers
and those who try to live and work by the seasons.

God of the harvest
God of the seas
forgive our greed,
our over-fishing
and needless killing for unnecessary delicacies,
our wastefulness.
Bless those who work on the seas:
sailors
fishermen and women
lifeboat crews
and those who try to live and work by the seasons.

God of the harvest
God of the skies
forgive our greed and pollution,
our desire for fast food delivery
and excessive travel across the globe,
our wastefulness.
Bless those who work in our skies:
pilots and air crews
helicopter crews.
Bless our fairtrade partners
and those who try to live and work by the seasons.

Make us ever mindful of the true cost to your creation:
of our disconnection to time and place

of our disconnection from the seasons you created
of our disconnection from you, Creator God.

We pray for reconciliation with the land, the seas and skies.
We pray for reconciliation between nations
and a genuine sharing of resources.
We pray for reconciliation between ourselves and our Creator.

We ask you to bless:
those who struggle to make a meagre living
from a famished and drought-ridden earth;
those who are made refugees
and are forced to live as strangers in lands without hope;
those in our own land who struggle to make ends meet
and are afraid for the future.

Creator God
reconnect us to your creation,
to its order and resources.

Redeemer God
reconcile us to your creation,
to each other and to you.

Spirit God
renew us to live within your creation,
aware of its seasons and our neighbours' needs.

God of the land
God of the seas
God of the skies

bless us
and make us a blessing
to those in need
within your created order. Amen

Ruth Bowen

STORY FROM ULVA:
THE YEAR THE POTATO WENT AWAY

The year the potato went away (*'A'bhlidhna a dh'fhalbh am buntata'*) – 1846 – was when the crop failed in Ulva. The large population – 500 people – who relied on potatoes for their existence, were faced with destitution and starvation, with no money to pay their rents and no other crop to feed themselves and their families. They survived on shellfish, dulse and other seaweed.

From Glasgow, a minister of St Columba's Gaelic Church, Dr Norman MacLeod (great-grandfather of George MacLeod, who founded the Iona Community) worked incessantly to relieve the sufferings of his fellow Highlanders, bringing their plight to the notice of the public, and collecting money and meal for their relief. He was called 'Friend of the Gaels'.

When he asked other ministers for information about the impact of the potato famine, one of the first to respond was the Rev William Fraser, minister of Ulva, who reported that the state of most of his parishioners was 'miserable beyond description'. The old hand-querns were being put to use to grind what corn remained. 'I believe,' he wrote that December, 'that it is beyond the power of many individuals to keep them-selves in life till summer.' He talked about whole families who had no food for days at a time. He believed that many would die.

Help was given in the short term, but in the next few years the potato famine, the collapse of the kelp industry and widespread poverty meant that many families were evicted and many then emigrated – except for the oldest and weakest who ended up on Starvation Terrace, the row of tiny cottages whose name says it all. A population of 500 was reduced to 150 in five years (by 1881 there were only 53 people living in Ulva). It wasn't just the potato that went away.

Jan Sutch Pickard

Based on information from 'As it were (Sin mar a bha), An Ulva Boyhood', by Donald W Mackenzie (Birlinn)

NOT SO SAFELY GATHERED IN

Not so safely gathered in,
in recent years.
Climate change, floods and disease
have taken their toll.

As we sing the joyful hymns
and admire the harvest display,
give us compassion
and understanding
which moves beyond our dismay
at the increased prices in our shops,
into prayer
and active concern
for those whose livelihood depends on the harvest
in all its forms.

We pray for farmers,
especially for those whose life's work has been destroyed in an instant;
for local people who suffer the knock-on effects;
for all affected by climate change across the world.

Carolyn Morris

21ST-CENTURY HARVEST

Lord, we give thanks for the changing of the seasons,
for autumn, the fullness of harvest
and the promise of rebirth and renewal,
for the fulfilment of our work
for goals achieved
for targets met and projects delivered.

Help us to celebrate what we have achieved.
Give us discipline to review our efforts
and the wisdom to learn from our mistakes.
Inspire us to plan ahead.

We ask this in the sure knowledge of the resurrection,
the transformation of death to new life,
and the building of your kingdom. Amen

Nick Burden

TWO HARVEST BLESSINGS

May God who supplies seeds to sow and bread to eat
supply us with all we need to produce a rich harvest.
MAY GOD BLESS ALL OUR WORK AND WORSHIP,
DONE IN CHRIST'S WAY AND FOR CHRIST'S GLORY,
TODAY AND EVERY DAY. AMEN

Lord of the harvest
who has given us so much;
help us to be generous like you,
that the world may know your goodness and blessing.
And may the blessing of God,
Maker, Son and Holy Spirit,
remain on us,
and be made known through us,
now and always. Amen

Simon Taylor

AUTUMN

GOD OF AUTUMN

God of autumn,
help us to be more like nature,
accepting the changing seasons;
like the changing of the trees:
not a dying as life sometimes feels,
but a stripping bare in preparation for inner growth,
knowing that to shed the outer layers
will reveal the strength that is hidden underneath.

God of autumn,
it's so hard to let things go:
the shields,
the camouflage,
the flimsy covers ...

We cannot hide from you;
you are our strength,
you see our inner beauty.
You see beyond the human dressings
and wish to clothe us in your love.

God of autumn,
help us to be more like nature,
accepting the changing seasons
not because they are out of our control,
but because they are in your hands.

Katrina Crosby

LETTING GO

The birch leaves are falling, Lord,
yellow diamonds on the green grass,
released in the autumn wind.
But I, Lord,
I still clutch tight the leaves of my old life,
useless, withered and dry.

Teach me to let go of the old –
old hurts and animosities, old troubles and grief.
Teach me to release them into the wind of your Spirit
to be whisked away,
that like the tree I may rest a while
at peace within,
then grow again in the spring.

Annie Heppenstall

CONKERS

You have always been good for me.
Yours is the brown mottled beauty
that has allowed me to say 'Wow!' and thank you,
to know that the leaves will come tumbling
that the wind will buffet
that the winter is near.

Yours too the legitimate outlet for anger,
the aim and the balance,
the energy of the downward smash
the bruising of fingers
the destruction
the victory
the permission to be vicious
to let the autumn tiger loose
to let the anger go.

You speak autumn to me
sticks and leaves
and childhood energy,
and the ripeness that this season offers
again and again.

Ruth Burgess

WALKS AND AUTUMN COLOURS

Dear God,
thank you for holidays and fun, wildlife and nature,
and for walks and autumn colours.
Thank you, O Lord, for holidays. Amen

Mary Sharples, aged 9

LORD JESUS, THANK YOU

Lord Jesus, thank you for our holidays, for fun, to run.
Thank you for walks and talks.
Thank you for all the nice colours on holidays,
and all the people who don't have them, we pray for.
Thank you for our holidays, this year, and the next? Amen

Annie Sharples, aged 8

PRAYER FOR AUTUMN

Lord of the seasons,
there is a time for dying
and a time for new birth;
a time to speak
and a time to keep quiet.
Help us discern your will for us now.

Lord of autumn leaves and warm berries,
help us to let go gracefully
and to rejoice in the colour and fruitfulness of this moment.
Wrap us in the shawl of eternity
and teach us to await with wonder
the new shoots of your love.

Mary Hanrahan

THE BLESSINGS OF AUTUMN

Group A: Creator God, we praise you for bright crisp mornings,
for leaves crackling underfoot
and wisps of cloud in a pale sky.

Group B: We praise you for the night-time rain,
for the wind buffeting the city
and streetlamps reflected in wet pavements.

Group A: We praise you for the season's labours,
for the smell of new-turned earth
and smoking bonfires.

Group B: We praise you for the season's gifts,
for fruitfulness beyond measure
and time to reflect and remember.

CREATOR GOD, WE PRAISE YOU.

Cally Booker

THANK YOU

Thank you
for the still, quiet woods of autumn,
carpets of shed acorns crunching underfoot,
mushrooms newly grown since yesterday
squatting among the gently shifting mosaic of fallen leaves.

For brown fields turned golden by the setting sun,
the cautious stare and stamping hooves of wary sheep,
the dapper magpie's raucous, laughing cry.

For hedgerows decorated purple, crimson, pink
by berries of bramble, bryony and spindle,
clusters of fluffy seeds released by willow herbs.

For all that has been grown, created and achieved this year,
as life settles to see out the winter's cold and storms
and waits to break out in new glories next year.

Brian Ford

LONG MEG DRUID CIRCLE

We are here at the dark end of summer;
on the rise, a harvester still packing in the sheaves.
High stinging nettles all in frills, brambles ripening,
crimson haw berries weighing down their still-green sleeves,
sycamores with yellowing clusters of autumnal leaves.
And on this ancient field, in uneven tufted grass,
sixty-nine extant stones, strange rocky humps
placed to form a circle by those Bronze Age farmers,
who relied on measuring the sun's angle
for their yearly working cycle.

Long Meg stands erect above the round.
On winter solstice, as the sun sets,
we are told, a golden halo
proves the time has come
to rest a while,
and celebrate.

Liz Gregory-Smith

THE LEAVES ARE AGEING

The leaves are ageing:
some rust

others seep yellow
through green

a few resist
this brittle change –

charge me with love
that I may fan

amber, red, crimson
into flame

then fall, light
as the skin of a chrysalis.

Mary Palmer

A PRAYER FOR LATE AUTUMN

Walk with us, God,
through sharp frosty days
and bright crunchy leaves
into winter.

Rest with us
by warm firesides
and tell us stories
into the night.

Take us out at night
and show us the stars
and fill us
with wonder.

Bless us and our families
our friends
and our neighbours
with love and with courage.

And never let us forget
the stranger
who needs to share our wealth,
our shelter
and our hope.

Ruth Burgess

ENVIRONMENT

THE WORLD IS YOURS

The world is yours, Lord,
in all its wonder and variety.
Help us to care for it and live on it responsibly;
to hold your gift with careful hands,
valuing land and creatures
and one another.

Margaret Harvey

WE ARE CONNECTED

We are sorry, Lord,
that just by living without thought
we pollute the air,
poison the waters
and damage the land.
We are sorry, Lord.

For we are connected,
whether we recognise it or not,
to all of creation;
to all that you made;
from ant to mountain
we are connected.

Holy Spirit,
heal and restore us,
that we may live gently on earth,
and all creation praise you,
the Living God,
Father, Son and Holy Spirit.

Chris Polhill

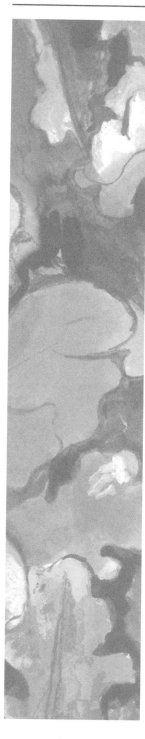

FAITH IN A NUTSHELL

(A meditation on a beech nut)

Inside
this prickly shell
silky soft skin
cups
the sharp-edged nut;
slowly
the petals of the pod
open
and release the promise
of new life.

In this sweet seed
hides
a great tree,
the mystery of its pattern
dispersed
into the rich earth
to disappear and grow
in secret;

to thrust bold shoots
through
the earth's crust,
until
the sturdy sapling stands
unshaken and unbent;
striving
towards its proud
and ancient heritage;
a blueprint
traced
in the beginning
of time,
when God
smiled.

Carol Dixon

STORM PRAYER

Through thunder
and lightning

the swell of waves
and slash of rain

the dark of doubt
and gales of grief

I believe, that You
walking on water

bring peace.

Mary Palmer

GLOBAL GARDEN

In Guinea-Bissau people scratch a living from tired earth
cash cropping for overfed northern markets.
In Somalia people carry muddy water for miles over arid desert tracks.
In Eritrea people pick over the bones of long-dead stock
for bitter herbs.

The closest I came
to taking responsibility
for what I ate
was hand picking
apples
from the shelves
of out-of-town
superstores.
Then I made a garden.

In my garden,
I dig till my back aches and my fingers blister,
I wage war against weather and weeds,
I compete with pests and pigeons,

I experience
success
and failure
in equal measure
not exactly famine
not exactly Eritrea
but maybe
just maybe
it brings me a
little closer
to an understanding
of what is
and what is not
important.

Pete Anderson

LET US BE LIKE YOU

Lord Jesus Christ,
you recognised the beauty of the lilies of the field.
In wild places you found the stillness
that helped you to pray.
You reminded us that every sparrow and raven
is known and cared for.
You saw the labour of the farmers
and enjoyed the fruit of that work.
Let us be like you and cherish this earth you created,
sustain and promise to make new.

Simon Taylor

THE HOLY WELL

The stone surround speaks
eloquently and authoritatively of centuries of liquid devotion.
And, but for the nearly-discreet surveillance camera,
you can be alone here with God and the water.
Light a candle, take your time,
read through the old prayer card
waterlogged, laminated
and hopelessly out of touch.

Who cares!
Don't be put off!
Faith transforms!
It's no delusion.

I once had the misfortune to talk with a civil engineer
(retired).
He sneered.
Some Holy Well.
It would have dried up long ago
when we widened the road
if we hadn't diverted the flow
to keep up appearances.

So what:
The water triumphs
Faith transforms
for description
is not explanation,
not by a long way.
And the wonder of the dark-cold water
is not quenched
by practicalities.
Have faith!

David Coleman

ENJOY THE EARTH GENTLY

Music: Alison Adam
Words: Yoruba poem

Sing unaccompanied with the cantor (leader) cueing the people. The song should be sung several times over, with the ending overlapping into the beginning. A light rainstick sound could finish the piece.

LIVING FLAME OF LOVE *

Living flame of love,
so touch our hearts with your bright fire,
that we of tepid, even chilly, faith,
may be alight with your passion,
and warm the globe with your love,
reflecting your care
for all of your creation. Amen

Chris Polhill

* A phrase from a prayer by St John of the Cross

STANDING ON THE EDGE

A liturgy

Opening responses

We are standing on the edge:
our Earth, the blue-green jewel we call home,
stands on the edge of global catastrophe.
Her green forests give way to charred blackened mess,
her blue skies stifled by smog,
her waters discoloured by filth,
her climate warming.
WE ARE STANDING ON THE EDGE.
THE EDGE OF LIFE – THE EDGE OF DEATH.

We are standing on the edge:
earth's creatures stand on the edge of extinction;
myriad species crafted by the hands of the Creator,
delighting Him with their diversity.
God's creatures vanish from the face of the earth,
and are lost
for ever.
WE ARE STANDING ON THE EDGE.
THE EDGE OF LIFE – THE EDGE OF DEATH.

We are standing on the edge:
creatures made in God's image and likeness
looking into the future with fear;
fear of inescapable debt,

fear of hunger and thirst.
Life lived, but always at the edges ...
WE ARE STANDING ON THE EDGE.
THE EDGE OF LIFE – THE EDGE OF DEATH.

We are standing on the edge:
creatures made in God's image and likeness
looking into the future with fear;
fear of poverty,
fear of homelessness and addiction.
Life lived, but always at the edges ...
WE ARE STANDING ON THE EDGE.
THE EDGE OF LIFE – THE EDGE OF DEATH.

We are standing on the edge:
creatures made in God's image and likeness
looking into the future with fear,
standing on the fringes of family life,
standing on the fringes of a prosperous society,
standing on the fringes of what is called 'normal'.
Life lived, but always at the edges ...
WE ARE STANDING ON THE EDGE.
THE EDGE OF LIFE – THE EDGE OF DEATH.

We will follow You, Lord.
We will go where You go
and see as You see.
But when we see a world filled with pain,
Lord, what hope is there?

Scripture reading: Luke 4:16–21

Action

The liturgy works well as a mini-pilgrimage. Select pictures from newspapers or magazines which reflect each of the different 'edges' – ecological damage, debt, hunger, homelessness ... Mount the pictures on card and stick them up in various places in the church/room or outside. As the service progresses, those gathered walk to stand before each image, and reflect on it and on the words they are hearing and saying.

Closing responses

Through Christ, the firstborn of all creation,
WE PRAY FOR RESPECT FOR THE EARTH

Through Christ, Prince of Peace,
WE PRAY FOR PEACE FOR EARTH'S PEOPLES

Through Christ, King of Love,
WE PRAY FOR LOVE IN OUR LIVES

Through Christ, Lord of the Dance,
WE PRAY FOR DELIGHT IN THE GOOD

Through Christ, Divine Healer,
WE PRAY FOR FORGIVENESS FOR PAST WRONGS

Through Christ, Morning Star rising over the world,
WE PRAY FOR THE GRACE TO MAKE A NEW START FOR OURSELVES
AND FOR OUR WORLD

And may God bless us and keep us, today and each day,
THE FATHER, THE SON AND THE HOLY SPIRIT,

And until we meet again
MAY GOD HOLD US IN THE PALM OF HIS HAND. AMEN

Wellspring

COLLECT FOR AGENDA 21*

O God, in love you created us
and in your grace you sustain us.
We thank you for all in creation that provides for our needs,
for all that is pleasing to our senses,
for all that is part of the web of life on planet Earth.
Help us to use wisely the resources of this earth:
to be willing to share and cooperate with others,
to pursue peace in all of our relationships,
to cherish all that your hands have made.
Help us to live responsibly
so that the earth may not only endure,
but flourish to the glory of your name. Amen

Simon Taylor

** Agenda 21 is a programme run by the United Nations relating to
sustainable development. 21 refers to the 21st century.*

A PRAYER FOR A 'WALKING BUS'

A walking bus is a supervised walk, usually to and from school, organised as an alternative to travelling by car or public transport. Parents and children join the 'bus' as it passes their home.

God our Creator,
protect our children
from idle car travel,
and cotton wool living.

May they enjoy
walking's freedom,
seeing the little things,
and fresh air living.

In the wonder
of your creating
may they notice you,
also beside them.

And adults too, Lord God.
May adults
notice you too.

Chris Polhill

O GOD, YOU ASKED

O God, you asked man and woman
to tend this garden of your creating,
to care for the creatures of your making.
We confess our failure,
and with shame acknowledge the damage we have done.
Forgive us, we pray,
and by your power at work in us
enable us to be wise guardians of creation
that this world may ever show your glory. Amen.

Simon Taylor

ALLOTMENTS

Past the pool table lawns, the paved paths and gravelled drives
at the end of the alleyway
are sagging wire fences,
erect leeks and onions in military rows,
home-made compost bins,
hedges of runner beans,
cloches made from discarded window glass
and pumpkins like rocs' eggs in straw and manure nests.
Here the growing of crops still needs sweaty brows:
stewards and Creator rub along together.

Brian Ford

WE THANK YOU FOR TREES

Dear God,
we thank you for trees;
for tall trees that seem to reach into the sky
yet are strong enough to stand against the storm.
We thank you for the fresh green leaves of spring
and the beautiful colours of autumn;
for the sound of the wind through the leaves;
for a place to shelter when the rain is falling;
for somewhere to play and hide.
We thank you for trees giving us oxygen to breathe,
and holding the soil together.
Thank you, God, for trees that give us fruit
and trees that give us wood to make things.
Thank you, God, that trees provide so many things for us;
help us always to care for them as you do. Amen

Simon Taylor

SACRAMENTS

DROPS

A drop of water from the sea,
where all life began,
on your forehead, beloved,
to pour abundant life into you
all the days to come.

A drop of water from the sky,
bringing relief to your parched soul,
on your forehead, my beloved,
that your spirit
will never thirst
for God's
grace.

A drop of water from my heart,
overflowing with joy,
on your forehead, our beloved,
so you feel God's hope
holding your hand
with every faltering step
you take.

One drop from the sea,
one drop from the sky,
one drop from my heart
mingle with Father, Son and Spirit,
the living waters
flowing with you
forever,

beloved of God.

Amen

Thom M Shuman

YOUR HEALING POWER

(Hosea 5:15–6:6; Matthew 9:9–13, 18–26)

Lord Jesus:
sinners, we follow you,
in faith, we reach for you.

In relationship, in community,
may we have courage
both to reach and to reveal,
to touch in one another
all that is shameful and hidden,
and so release
the merciful light of your healing power.
Amen

Julie Greenan

A PENITENTIAL LITURGY

A penitential service is traditionally held in the days before a major feast, particularly Christmas or Easter Day. This liturgy can be augmented by a homily and hymns, or parts of it can be used within a wider context. It can be used with a large congregation, a small group, or with an individual and their soul friend. An optional act of contrition is included. Possible hymns and readings are included in the notes.

Opening responses

Whoever we are
Whatever we've done
GOD LOVES US

When our hands are clean
When our hands are dirty
GOD LOVES US

God tells us to listen to Jesus
GOD OFFERS US FORGIVENESS AND A NEW START

Readings *(see notes)*

For the Word of God in scripture,
for the Word of God among us,

for the Word of God within us,
THANKS BE TO GOD

Prayer of confession

We are made in God's image.
God loves us.
Let us bring ourselves and our concerns to God ...

(time of silence)

For the people I have hurt
I'M SORRY
For the mistakes I have made
I'M SORRY
For the things I didn't do
I'M SORRY
For hurting myself
I'M SORRY

GOD OF LOVE AND MERCY,
FORGIVE ME.
HELP ME TO LET GO OF MY HURT AND REGRET.

Act of contrition *(see notes)*

Letting go of someone or something: unknotting rope
Laying down something/letting go of someone: putting a stone at the foot of a cross
Washing clean: washing hands

Absolution

(The words of Jesus can be read by one voice, or by three different voices.)

GOD,
I HAVE DONE WHAT I CAN TO CHANGE DIRECTION.
I KNOW THAT MY PAST IS PART OF ME
AND SO IS YOUR HEALING LOVE.
I ASK YOU FOR FORGIVENESS AND A CLEAN START.
LET ME HEAR NOW
YOUR WORDS OF FORGIVENESS AND HOPE:

Jesus said:
'Come to me, you who are heavy laden
and I will give you rest.'

Jesus said:
'Your sins are forgiven you.
Go and sin no more.'

Jesus said:
'Don't be afraid, I love you.
Come and follow me.'

THANKS BE TO GOD. AMEN

Lighting a candle

Either light a central candle, or take light from a central candle to light individual candles.

As God's children
we will walk in the light.

Light candle/s

JESUS IS THE LIGHT OF THE WORLD.
JESUS IS THE LIGHT OF OUR LIVES.

Travelling on

Who we were
and what we've done
is safe with God.
WHO WE ARE NOW
AND WHO WE WILL BECOME
IS SAFE WITH GOD

May the blessing of God,
Maker, Jesus and Holy Spirit,
be on us and in us always.
MAY WE TRAVEL HOMEWARDS
IN JUSTICE AND IN LOVE. AMEN

NOTES

Readings

Psalm 51:1–2,10–12
Psalm 86:4–7
Hosea 11
Micah 6:8
Mark 2:15–17
John 3:16–21
John 8:1–11
Romans 8:38–39

Readings from sources other than scripture can be used.

Act of contrition

Individuals can be invited to symbolise their contrition if they would find this helpful. Within a congregational context, the symbols used should be placed in different parts of the building. A cross should be placed centrally.

(i) Untying a knot in a piece of rope/cord – to symbolise letting go of someone/something that has hurt them. Pieces of rope/cord, about a foot-long each, tied with one knot, are placed upon a table. After an individual has untied their knot, they can take the untied piece of rope and lay it at the foot of the cross.

(ii) Laying down a stone – to symbolise putting down a burden. A table with a number of stones is needed. An individual can pick up a stone and take it to the cross and leave it there.

(iii) Washing hands – to symbolise washing away dirt and evil. A table with a large bowl/s of clean water and towels are needed. At the end of the act of contrition the bowls and towels are carried to and left at the foot of the cross.

Background music could be played during the act of contrition.

Possible hymns (from Church Hymnary 4):
97 (Psalm 139) O God, you search me and you know me
115 Love is the touch of intangible joy
386 Lifted high on your cross
482 Come, let us to the Lord our God
493 It's me, O Lord
540 I heard the voice of Jesus say
726 When we are living, we are in the Lord
789 Now go in peace

Ruth Burgess

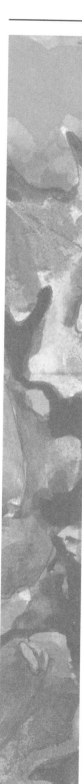

COMPASSIONATE GOD

Compassionate God,
in a world which is broken,
in communities which are divided,
with lives that are wounded –
we turn to you for healing.
We open our hearts to you
and receive encouragement;
we listen to your word
and find meaning;
we stretch out our hands to you
and find wholeness. Amen

Jan Sutch Pickard

LORD, HAVE MERCY

Let us open our lives to God and ask for his forgiveness and grace ...

Silence

On the poverty of our seeing and on the poverty of our believing,
Lord, have mercy.
LORD, HAVE MERCY.

On the poverty of our giving and on the poverty of our following,
Christ, have mercy.
CHRIST, HAVE MERCY.

On the poverty of our loving and on the poverty of our living,
Lord, have mercy.
LORD, HAVE MERCY.

To all who turn to him, Christ says, 'Your sins are forgiven.'
He also says, 'Follow me.'
AMEN. THANKS BE TO GOD.

David Hamflett

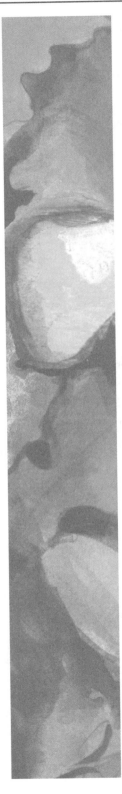

YOU TOUCHED ME THEN

(A meditation)

When I fell, I grazed my knee
or banged my head
or hurt my arm.
You put on a plaster
or rubbed it better
and told me it would be all right.
You touched me then
and as you did, so did Christ.

When I was in pain,
you used your skill
and applied your fingers
and manipulated my body
until you made it right.
You touched me then
and as you did, so did Christ.

When there was something wrong
and part of my body would not work
or was causing distress,
you tested and probed
and used your skill with a scalpel.
With my body in your hands
you touched me then
and as you did, so did Christ.

When I was depressed
and life was dark and empty,
you put your arms around me
and told me you loved me
and kindled a light within my soul.
You touched me then
and as you did, so did Christ.

When I was in anguish,
watching a loved one suffer,
stunned by disappointment,
expecting bad news,
you sat with me holding my hand,
supporting me with your silent touch,
and told me it would be all right.

You touched me then
and as you did, so did Christ.

When grief was raw
and my life blown apart,
you held me while I cried a river
of tears into your shoulder
till I could weep no more.
You touched me then
and as you did, so did Christ.

When life was a burden
and work was stressful,
or things had not worked out as planned,
or my body was never going to work properly again,
or grief and disappointment still nagged,
you touched my shoulder,
letting me know that you understood.
You touched me then
and as you did, so did Christ.

When I come to worship
bringing all my needs and concerns,
which you may or may not know,
and do not always need to know,
you take my hands in yours.
You say, 'The peace of the Lord',
God's healing shalom.
You touch me then
and as you do, so does Christ.

When I come to your table
with my faults and my fears,
my needs and my hurts,
just 'me' as I am now,
holding out my open hands,
I feel the touch of bread.
I know your acceptance of this 'me' that I am.

When others touched me, so you did then.
As bread touches me, so you do now.
You touch me,
O Christ, and make me whole.

David Hamflett

GOD, WE ARE HERE

(A prayer of approach)

God, we are here,
we have come into this church to meet with you;
we are here as your family,
here because this is where we need to be,
together seeking your wholeness and love.

God, we need you:
when faced with a choice between good and evil,
we choose the things that harmed us and those around us,
we have failed to love other people,
we've held grudges,
we've ignored injustice,
we have been jealous and unforgiving.

God, we're ashamed,
we want to run away from you, to curl up somewhere and hide,
and yet,
as we turn to go,
we hear you calling us back,
calling us by name.

And so we are here, God,
some of us are angry, some of us are afraid,
but we're here,
and we tell you in the silence the kind of people that we really are,
and we tell you that we're sorry.

(Short silence)

God, have mercy on us.
Christ, have mercy on us.

Listen then to Jesus,
feel his touch, know his love,
for through him God says to us:
'Your sins are forgiven, you are loved,
you are free.'

God, thank you. Amen

Ruth Burgess

GLORIA

Tune: The Ash Grove (Welsh traditional)

All glory to God in the heights of the heavens,
and peace to his people, his people on earth;
we praise you, we bless you, we give you our worship,
and for your great glory we sing out our thanks.
O Lord, heavenly King, God the Father Almighty,
Lord Jesus the Christ and the Father's dear Son,
Lord God, Lamb of God, only Son of the Father
have mercy on us, Lord, have mercy on us.

Lord, you take away all the sin of the world,
hear our prayer from your place at the Father's right hand;
have mercy upon us; you only are holy
and you, you alone, are our Lord and our God.
Lord Christ, Holy Spirit and Father Almighty,
most high and most glorious, we give you our praise.
All glory to God in the heights of the heavens,
and peace to his people, his people on earth.

Margaret Harvey

WHAT KIND OF A GOD?

ALL: WE BELIEVE IN GOD
Child: What kind of a God?

Voice A: A creative God who made the stars and spiders.
Voice B: A warm God who is bright and full of colour.
Voice C: A God who is our friend, who loves us and knows us by name.

ALL: WE BELIEVE IN JESUS
Child: What is he like? Tell me about him.

Voice A: He was exciting. He told lots of stories. He made people laugh and smile.
Voice B: He reached out to people: he listened to them and helped them.
Voice C: He asked people questions: he challenged them, made them think.
Voice A: Some people didn't like Jesus. They told lies about him and he was sentenced to death and killed.
Voice B: But God, the Father, brought Jesus back to life again.
Voice C: Following Jesus is an adventure, a journey, a good surprise.

ALL: WE BELIEVE IN THE HOLY SPIRIT
Child: What's that?

Voice A: Maybe 'who's that?'.
Voice B: Someone who brings us to God.
Voice C: Someone who lets us know how much God loves us.
Voice A: Someone we can't see but can feel.
Voice B: Like the wind blowing our hair.
Voice C: Like the warmth of a candle flame.

ALL: WE BELIEVE IN THE CHURCH
Child: This church or the one down the road?

Voice A: Every church, all of them together.
Voice B: Not the buildings, but all the people who love God.
Voice C: All of us working together with God to make the world beautiful.

ALL: WE BELIEVE GOD CALLS US
Child: To do what?

Voice A: To love all people.
Voice B: To forgive them when they hurt us.
Voice C: To trust and not be afraid.
Voice A: To help make the world the place God wants it to be.
Voice B: To care for the world and enjoy it.

Voice C:	Amen.
Child:	Pardon?
Voice A:	Amen. It means – so be it – OK – let it happen.
Child:	Oh! OK – Amen.
ALL:	AMEN

Ruth Burgess

JESUS CALLS US TO HIS TABLE

(Tune: All for Jesus)

Jesus calls us to his table
with the last and lost and least,
offering us his very nature –
come and celebrate the feast!

He took bread, gave thanks and broke it,
shared it with his chosen friends,
instituted this memorial
to a truth that never ends.

In the same way after supper
offered them the cup of wine,
symbol of eternal giving
trodden from the living vine.

Here our thanks and praise we offer,
as we take this hallowed bread,
as we drink the wine of heaven,
as we each in turn are fed.

Living Jesus, so impel us
with your free converting grace,
that this Eucharist may lead us
to the edge of time and space.

Josie Smith

LAMB OF GOD

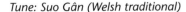

Tune: *Suo Gân (Welsh traditional)*

Jesus, Lamb of God, have mercy,
Lord, have mercy on us.
Jesus, bearer of our sins,
Lord, have mercy on us.
Jesus, Jesus, world's Redeemer,
Jesus, give to us your peace.
Jesus, Lamb of God, have mercy,
Lord, have mercy on us.

Margaret Harvey

WE GIVE THANKS

(Prayers of thanksgiving and intercession)

We give thanks for the beauty of God's creation:
for the glory we see around us
for the mystery of wonder and life
for green leaves, bird song, and smiles of wonder.
Thank you, God
THANK YOU, GOD

We give thanks for the friendship of Jesus:
for the stories he told
for the hope that he gives us
for good Samaritans, broken bread and laughter.
Thank you, God
THANK YOU, GOD

We give thanks for the work of the Holy Spirit:
for the wisdom and challenges she brings
and the courage she gifts us

for wild dances, shared tears, and new adventures
Thank you, God
THANK YOU, GOD

We pray for our world, for those who suffer because of climate change,
for those who are afraid of what tomorrow may bring.
We pray for those who seek to renew the seas and the earth,
for botanists, for marine biologists and for growers of flowers, vegetables and fruit.
In our community we pray for ......
God in your mercy
HEAR OUR PRAYER

We pray for people who live in places of war and conflict,
for fighters, child soldiers, for those who get hurt.
And we pray for all who work to bring peace and justice,
for volunteers and peace builders,
for those who seek to do good to everyone.
In our community we pray for ......
God in your mercy
HEAR OUR PRAYER

We pray for people who are homeless
and for those who are living in places that are strange to them,
for new people in our churches, for new children in our classroom,
for those who are living away from people they love.
And we pray for all who welcome strangers and offer hospitality,
who listen and befriend.
In our community we pray for ......
God in your mercy
HEAR OUR PRAYER

We pray for the church, for the church that is organisation and buildings,
for the church that is projects and people;
we pray for ourselves.
God in your mercy
HEAR OUR PRAYER

God of grace and mercy,
hear our prayers
both those spoken and those held in our hearts;
we ask them in Jesus's name
and in the power of the Holy Spirit.
AMEN

Ruth Burgess

COMMUNION FOR KIDS

God be with you.
AND WITH YOU.

Open your hearts.
WE OPEN THEM TO GOD.

We say thank you to God.
WE ALWAYS WANT TO THANK GOD FOR EVERYTHING.

Prayer

Bunnies and butterflies,
dogs with muddy feet,
cats with whiskers that tickle,
frogs that jump a mile,
worms inching along the pavement,
you made all this –
and so much more:
skies so blue we want to dive in,
fluffy clouds to pillow our dreams,
mums who throw us high in the air,
dads who hold us when we are scared.
You made all this,
and so, so much more,
for us!
Thank you, God!

And hear us as we sing with the angels
and all your children.

Song: Jesus Loves Me (two verses)

Prayer

God, you loved your child, Jesus,
and could have kept him close to you,
but you sent him to show us your love.

A little boy, he skinned his knees playing
and liked his mum and dad to read him stories.
A teenager, he felt sort of clumsy,
and wondered what he would do
when he grew up.
When he got older,

he was a friend to people
who felt no one liked them;
he loved the people
everyone else picked on;
he would gather up kids on his lap,
and tell them
how much God loved them.
Then he died,
for his friends,
and for those who didn't like him.
That's when God,
who loved his child so much,
brought him back to life,
just as God will give us
new life when we die.

And so, we sing about Jesus,
God's child, our friend, our Saviour.

Song: Away in the Manger (two verses)

Prayer

You blow through the trees,
making the leaves dance;
you cool us off
on a hot summer day;
you whisper in our ears
about God's dreams for us.
So come now, Spirit of God,
and make this bread
we are about to eat
taste so good we want
to share it with everyone we meet.
Make the juice in the cup
so sweet and pure
that we want to go out
and tell others about God's love.

Thank you, Jesus, for loving us so much;
thank you, Spirit, for helping us so much;
thank you, God, for being with us,
now and for ever. Amen

Thom M Shuman

FOUR COMMUNION PRAYERS

Let the people come
to our hearts' true allegiance;
beyond family and land,
beyond kingdoms and powers,
beyond time and self,
may Love draw and shape us;
through bread, wine and one another,
make us your body, your people. Amen

Come to the heart of Christ,
where all are one:
receive the extravagant gift
which alone expects nothing in return;
through the boundless hospitality of the Spirit.
Come, taste God,
lover and beloved.

In this Holy Communion,
find healing, rest and release;
in one another,
find love for body, mind and spirit;
come home to God
and be at peace.

Spirit of love unknown,
here are bread, wine and our fractured lives:
the random blows and the familiar struggles;
friendship and kindness, hope and hospitality.
In trust, we offer all that we are,
to you and to one another.
Out of condemnation, draw compassion,
out of suffering, solidarity,
and through this bread and wine,
make love in action. Amen

Julie Greenan

SOURCE OF ALL LIFE

(Tune: Jerusalem, adapted for three verses, CH4 106)

Source of all life, Eternal Now,
guardian of all that's yet to be,
maker of all, above, below,
great Lord of heaven and earth and sea,
from this your feast of love and care
we rise to sing our songs of praise
for grace abounding everywhere,
for love surrounding all our days.

Lord Jesus Christ, Eternal Word
cradled in flesh before our sight,
bone of our bone, our servant Lord,
yet filled with heaven's all glorious light,
from this your feast of love and care
we rise to be your body now.
In all our living, everywhere,
give to us grace to keep our vow.

Spirit of God, Eternal Breath,
both wind and fire of peace and love,
bringer of life, stronger than death,
the life in which we daily move,
from this your feast of love and care
we rise with minds and hearts ablaze
to seek your presence everywhere,
and find, in all our living, praise.

Leith Fisher

THREE PRAYERS FOR SENDING OUT

Holy God,
in Jesus, we see your meaning and nature;
may we follow him inward
to find ourselves held
in the infinite spaciousness of the soul.
And may we go out with him,
our poor selves stumbling in his footsteps,
not seeking perfection in vain,
but coming to know that
all is well, even the worst:
for in God, everything belongs. Amen

Jesus, Lord:
give us faith and courage
to rise to your impossible challenge;
send us out
to act with vigour and purpose,
trusting not in our wisdom,
but moving in your grace;
trusting not in our words
but surrendering to the Spirit of truth. Amen

Spirit of questioning hearts,
hopeful and afraid,
we wait to recognise you.
Bless our doubt and our disbelief;
may we share both our uncertainty and our conviction,
and inspire one another
to go out, as we are,
and act in the name of Christ risen. Amen. Alleluia

Julie Greenan

GOD SENDS US OUT

God sends us out into the world –

not to build walls
but to dismantle barriers.

Not to load on chains
but to liberate the oppressed.

Not to close our doors
but to welcome in the stranger.

Not to further fragment the body of Christ
but to re-imagine it.

God sends us out into the world
to live as a sign
of the justice and peace
of his kingdom.

Pat Bennett

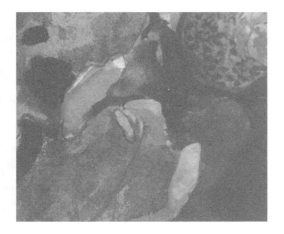

PEACE AND JUSTICE

DAILY BREAD

God surrounded by glory:
you notice the people we walk past,
and journey with them
wherever they are going.
You speak out for the voiceless
and try to open our ears to their cries.

Jesus, Healer of the hopeless,
converser with the outsider:
In you,
faith and works walk hand in hand
down the streets of the kingdom.
In you,
the have-a-lots and the have-nothings
find themselves sitting
side by side at your table,
passing grace to one another.
In you,
those with good names
and those with no names
are called by one name:
Beloved.

Spirit of Compassion:
sow justice in our hearts
that the poor might find in us
a friend;
sow peace in our spirits,
that the angry might find in us
a sea of hope;
sow generosity in our hands,
that the hungry might find in us
their daily bread.

Thom M Shuman

A SAFE CITY

(Zechariah 8:1–19)

Do you have
a dream of
a safe city?

My favourite
is the one
God shares with Zechariah,
a place where
old people,
who use walking sticks,
sit and talk
in city squares,
and the streets
are full
of children playing.

When the streets
are unsafe
I try to be brave
and to act justly,
and to hold on
to God's dream.

Ruth Burgess

PRODIGAL GOD

Prodigal God:
you set before us not merely sufficient, but limitless abundance.
You do not wish for us deprivation and a meagre ration,
but the glorious excess of life itself;
fill us, then, with such sweet hunger
that we shall not rest
until we sit down with the oppressed
to share and savour the bread of liberation. Amen

Julie Greenan

PEACE AND JUSTICE PRAYERS FROM KILCHATTAN PRIMARY SCHOOL

(Isle of Colonsay, Argyll)

Dear God,
please help the poor people in the world
and answer their prayers. Amen

Dear God,
could you stop murders and fights?
Thanks.

Dear God,
help all the people in the world
and help us
stop global warming.

Dear God,
stop wars
Amen

READING SCRIPTURE

O Prophet and Teacher,
who proclaimed good news for the poor,
come, teach us your way of reading scripture.

Penny Seabrook

PRAYERS OF INTERCESSION FOR RACIAL JUSTICE SUNDAY

Jesus, you taught us that humanity is one.
We've grown to more than 7 billion people on this earth –
sisters and brothers in God's rainbow of cultures and ethnicities.
God, help us to celebrate our diversity and open our hearts to all.
Encourage us not to just rest in the familiar, the tribe, the things we love and know.

Racial justice is not near at hand.
Lord, we have a very long way to go.
As Britain's thousands of mixed-raced children grow into adulthood,
they witness our range of cultures as rigid and separated,
with few signs of reconciliation.

Lord, we pray for the English school kids in Scotland
who get punched in the face for being English.
We pray for the Pakistani corner shop owner
who gets targeted and robbed because he is seen as an easy target.
We pray for young black people
who continually get pulled over and searched by the police for driving a posh car.

Lord, we pray for children of all races growing up in Britain.
We pray for elders of every culture and race.

Jesus, you knew all about mixed communities and racial injustice.
Two thousand years ago the sign on the cross above your head
was written in three languages so that everyone in the land could understand it.
JESUS, LIVE THROUGH US AS WE WALK YOUR PATH
OF RECONCILIATION AND JUSTICE FOR ALL.

Jesus, when racial identities clash we can hold on to our own beliefs so tightly
that we no longer have a hand free to extend love to others.
JESUS, LIVE THROUGH US AS WE WALK YOUR PATH
OF RECONCILIATION AND JUSTICE FOR ALL.

Jesus, help us to find our strength in you as we open our lives to embrace difference.
JESUS, LIVE THROUGH US AS WE WALK YOUR PATH
OF RECONCILIATION AND JUSTICE FOR ALL. AMEN

Simon de Voil

THROUGH OUR MUTUAL LOVE SOW FREEDOM

God of grace,
you call us to live by grace:
teach us how to do so,
in our personal lives,
in our community,
in the wider world.
THROUGH OUR MUTUAL LOVE SOW FREEDOM

God of peace,
you call us to be peacemakers:
teach us how to do so,
in our personal lives,
in our community,
in the wider world.
THROUGH OUR MUTUAL LOVE SOW FREEDOM

God of wisdom,
you call us to be wise:
teach us how to be so,
in our personal lives,
in our community living,
in the wider world.
THROUGH OUR MUTUAL LOVE SOW FREEDOM

God of gentleness,
you call us to be gentle:
teach us how to be so,
in our personal lives,
in our community living,
in the wider world.
THROUGH OUR MUTUAL LOVE SOW FREEDOM

God of creation,
you call us to be creative:
teach us how to be so,
in our personal lives,
in our community living,
in the wider world.
THROUGH OUR MUTUAL LOVE SOW FREEDOM

God of generosity,
you call us to be generous:
teach us how to be so,
in our personal lives,
in our community living,
in the wider world.
THROUGH OUR MUTUAL LOVE SOW FREEDOM

God of love,
you call us to be loving:
teach us how to be so,
in our personal lives,
in our community living,
in the wider world.
THROUGH OUR MUTUAL LOVE SOW FREEDOM

God of passion,
you call us to be passionate for justice:
teach us how to be so,
in our personal lives,
in our community living,
in the wider world.
THROUGH OUR MUTUAL LOVE SOW FREEDOM

Elizabeth Baxter

WHY?

Dear God,
why do people pinch?

Kerry

INTERCESSIONS BEFORE AN ELECTION

Loving God
whose spirit is truth;
revealing,
unmasking.

In this election week
help us to listen for your voice through the clamour of competing slogans;
to discern the right choice for our precious vote,
so that when we say what we want for the future of our country
we might speak the truth,
your holy truth,
in a spirit of justice and compassion.

Loving God
whose spirit is truth;
uplifting,
enlightening.

Help us to listen for the voices of the people
whose concerns are seldom heard on our political stage;
those who carry labels not of their own making –
'asylum seeker', 'economic migrant', 'socially excluded' ...
Help us to challenge what we hear
and not to accept what we know to be unjust,
to lift off the labels and see the real people,
people made in your divine image,
and to hear what they have to say.

Loving God,
whose spirit is truth;
everlasting,
untiring.

You have been patient with our persistent, carefully nurtured ignorance,
our determination to keep our heads in the sand
and pretend that doing nothing is different from doing harm.
But you are calling us to begin again,
to change ourselves,
to do good,

to speak the truth
and to live in love.

Loving God,
you have promised that your spirit will always be with us
and we put our trust in you. Amen

Cally Booker

TURNING THE WORLD UPSIDE DOWN

Voice 1:   Experienced adult-thinking rules!
Voice 2:   You know it makes sense, if you're honest.
Voice 3:   Unless you become childlike, you cannot enter God's kingdom.
Voice 4:   What nonsense!

Voice 1:   We must budget to annihilate the enemy as a necessary defence
in the balance of power.
Voice 2:   You know it makes sense, if you're honest.
Voice 3:   'Put away your sword.' God's power is vulnerable and gentle.
Voice 4:   What nonsense!

Voice 1:   Buy now, while our currency is strong. It's purchasing power which counts
in the end.
Voice 2:   You know it makes sense, if you're honest.
Voice 3:   Share freely so that each person's real needs are justly met.
Voice 4:   What nonsense!

Voice 1:   We hold the truth. God is on our side.
Voice 2:   You know it makes sense, if you're honest.
Voice 3:   God is to be found in every person, in every religion, in every race,
in every nation.
Voice 4:   What nonsense!

David Hawkey

BRING US TO SILENCE

O God,
bring us to silence
that we may hear your voice
in those calling from the edge.
Move us to stand with them
in speechless solidarity;
write your love on our bodies
that our living, not our lips,
may sing your freedom song. Amen

Julie Greenan

INTERCESSIONS FOR A TWIN CITY CELEBRATION

Living God,
we offer you our prayers for this precious planet.
We praise you for its diverse beauty:
mountains and plains,
lochs and deserts,
oceans and seashore;
and we thank you for its life-sustaining powers
which we too often abuse, forgetful of future generations.
Give us the wisdom and the courage to challenge
the pattern of exploitation and damage,
and the grace to live more gently on the earth.

Lord, in your mercy,
HEAR OUR PRAYER

Living God,
gathered here from cities east and west,
we offer you our prayers for these vibrant and diverse communities
where all aspects of human life –
industry and commerce, science and the arts,
education, healthcare, families and friendships –
jostle and sparkle together,
drawing people in to work and to live.
We thank you for the opportunities which city life can bring
and pray that we will not forget those for whom they are out of reach.

Make us sensitive to the needs of the vulnerable in our communities
and help us to shape a safe and inclusive environment
where all are welcomed, valued and enabled.

Lord, in your mercy,
HEAR OUR PRAYER

Living God,
gathered here in celebration
we offer you our prayers for those who have little reason to rejoice.
We call to mind ...

We thank you for all who work to ease distress in troubled situations:
the negotiators and rescue workers,
the doctors, nurses and counsellors.
Through the support of all who help and pray
may those in need feel the touch of your Holy Spirit
and be refreshed and restored.

Lord, in your mercy,
HEAR OUR PRAYER

All these prayers we offer to you, Living God,
in the name of Jesus Christ, our strength and our hope. Amen

Cally Booker

TREASURE ON EARTH

(A dialogue)

Sometimes we find it hard to identify with Jesus's teaching on wealth and poverty, because it seems to relate to extremes that are not part of our experience. This dialogue was used in a service to encourage people to think about 'The parable of the rich fool' (Luke 12:13–21). Adapt the dialogue to your own context!

I'm not wealthy, but I suppose I'm reasonably well-off. I live in a nice house and the mortgage is nearly paid off.

I'm not poor, but sometimes I feel a bit hard-up. I live in a nice house, but it's a struggle to keep on top of the mortgage payments and the repairs.

I shop at Sainsbury's and Marks & Spencer's, or the farmers' market for dinner parties, and stock up on organic stuff whenever I can.

I usually go to Asda – they have some great offers, and I always look to see what they've reduced because it's nearing its sell-by date. Sometimes friends come round for a takeaway and a few beers.

I can't afford luxury holidays, but we try to rent a villa somewhere sunny every summer, and usually fit in a city break as well. Of course, I pay to offset my carbon emissions.

I can't afford expensive holidays, but I usually take the kids camping or to a caravan. Sometimes we even manage to get a last-minute package deal somewhere hot and sunny.

I'm not wealthy, and sometimes the school fees are a bit of a struggle – but it's worth a few sacrifices to make sure they get the best possible education. And of course they all play an instrument, and the cost of lessons mounts up.

My kids go to the local comprehensive – they're all doing well – but the costs of uniforms and trips really stretch my budget. They love playing computer games, but it's hard trying to give them the latest versions to keep up with their friends.

Of course it's expensive trying to run two cars, but really we both need them for work. The children are always wanting lifts – and the People carrier is so useful when we go away.

I use the bus for work, but I'm trying to keep my old banger on the road – it's great for trips out with the kids at weekends.

I have a good job, with a pension, but I've invested in a personal pension plan as well – it seemed only sensible.

I should get a small pension from work, but otherwise it's relying on the state pension.

I save regularly through ISAs and building society accounts – I need to think of the future for myself and my family.

I try to put away a little bit each week, and put all my loose change in the piggy bank. Sometimes I worry about the future, but I'll just have to hope I win the lottery!

I'm not wealthy, but I do try to be a good steward of my money. I have a number of regular standing orders to charity, and gift-aid my donations whenever I can.

I don't have a lot, but I do like to try to help out – always buy a Big Issue, and put something in the collecting box for charity.

Of course I don't believe in being materialistic, and laying up treasure on earth – but it's right to be prudent and responsible with my money, isn't it?

I don't think I'm materialistic, but it would be nice to be able to store up a bit of treasure on earth, wouldn't it?

Jan Berry and Alma Fritchley

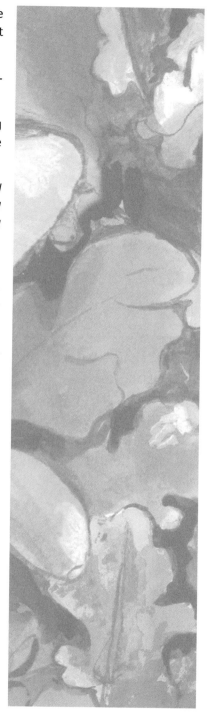

DAILY LIFE

WHAT DO YOU DO?

(A conversation for two voices)

What do you do?
Engineer?
Miner?
Road sweeper?
Policeman?

But what if you don't?
Maybe you're not,
you can't,
you won't.
Probably you aren't even.
How can you be, when you don't?
But I say
don't listen to them if you don't,
you still are.

Make a list of what you are:

man
husband
father

OK, go on
there's much more.

gardener
naturalist
believer
lover

Don't stop, you're winning.

neighbour
carer
laugher
wit.
Is that it?

No! Go on!

drinker
mate

storyteller
gourmet.
Will that do?

No. Go on!

I can't think any more.
I just know I don't
so I feel I'm not …
Who cares for all that?

You do, you know,
and so do I.
God does too!
Don't deny those 15 things!

Just add a few more
each time the world says,
'You don't, so you aren't.'

Just say:
'But I do and I am,
though not quite in your way.'

OK, so I am.
But I still wish that I did.
I still need the label
and the money it brings.

Judy Dinnen

ON OUR JOURNEY

God, who made the heavens,
let us know today that you are with us.
Like a bird in her nest, protecting,
warming and feeding her small ones,
so much more are you watching over us.
When we fall let us be aware that wherever we are on our journey,
we are held safely in your hands.

Sofia Adrian

SMALL GESTURES

Thank you, God,
for small gestures:
for an acorn squash left on the doorstep,
for an unexpected card in the mail,
for encouraging email,
for cats that sneak in with a smug look,
for music that touches the soul,
for cups of tea,
for ladybirds on the windowsill,
for wind chimes.

Thank you, God,
that, when life gets overwhelming,
you send kindness through friend, stranger and nature;
that when life feels like it's swirling out of control,
you have us held in the palm of your hand.

Katrina Crosby

A PLAYFUL LITURGY

Call to worship

Give thanks to God!
WE THANK GOD FOR THE JOY OF JUMPING ROPE,
AND THE LAUGHTER IN PLAYING LEAPFROG!

Give thanks to God at all times!
WE THANK GOD FOR THE COOL WATERS
OF A POOL ON A HOT SUMMER DAY –
AND THE WAY THE WATER SURPRISES US
WHEN WE FIRST JUMP IN!

Give thanks to God at all times and for all things!
WE THANK GOD FOR FIREFLIES
MAKING OUR NIGHTS BRIGHTER,
AND FOR BUTTERFLIES
WHICH TICKLE US AWAKE FROM A NAP.

Prayer

Every day is a day of wonder –
filled with empty cardboard boxes
which can take us to the moon,
and long afternoon ball games
where the score is never kept.
You rub the sleep from our eyes
so we can see you at play,
in the children on the corner,
in the teenager balancing on a skateboard,
in the old couple waltzing the night away:
Every day is a day of wonder,
Imaginative God

Every day is a day of laughter –
from the cereal which crackles us awake,
to the cat stalking the sunbeam;
from the baby just discovering her toes,
to the old man who puts sacks of tomatoes
on his neighbours' porches;
from the hummingbird drinking nectar,
to the dog grabbing the hose out of our hand:
Every day is a day of laughter,
Smiling Christ.

Every day is a day of joy.
We hear the squeals of children
jumping on the trampoline,
and the sweet sound of a ball
off the bat down at the playground.
We hope no one sees us
as we try out the hopscotch
drawn on the pavement,
and we smile from our porch
at the father putting training wheels
on his daughter's bike.
We put yesterday out with the garbage,
and wait for the delivery of tomorrow –
and we discover that
every day is a day of joy,
Spirit of Gladness.

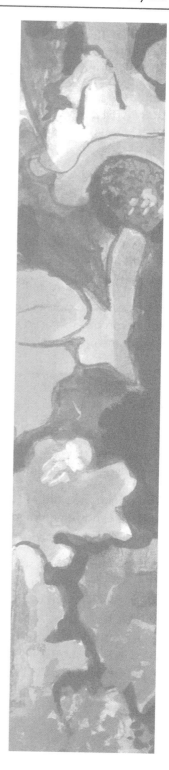

Help us to play with you
each and every day,
God in Community, Holy and One.

Help us to pray
OUR FATHER ...

Call to reconciliation

In a world which teaches us always to be serious,
God gives us
children who love to make silly faces.

In a world which searches for perfection,
God hands us
the platypus.

Let us speak to God of our reluctance to be playful,
so we can be embraced by the One who was willing to put aside divine dignity
to become one of us.

Prayer of confession

God of Wonder, you take mud, add a little water, and make mountains,
while we worry about getting our clothes dirty playing with our kids.

You nourish your creation with refreshing rain,
and we grumble about leaving our umbrellas at home.

You grin at the sight of squirrels chasing one another up and down trees,
and we can't remember the last time we lay on the grass,
trying to picture what the clouds up in the sky look like.

We take ourselves so seriously that we lose sight
of the wonder of your gifts.
We think you want us to be serious all the time,
and we have forgotten the joy, the laughter, the delight
which Jesus Christ, our Lord and Saviour, brought into our lives.
FORGIVE US, IMAGINATION BEHIND CREATION,
FOR FORGETTING TO ENJOY, TO LAUGH, TO PLAY.

Silence

Assurance of pardon

The good news is this: imagination and play
go hand in hand with prayer, with service,
with worship, with life.
God takes delight when we take the time
to enjoy and play in the good creation
offered to us. Amen

Thom M Shuman

LORD OF THE SINGING SPHERES

Lord of the singing spheres
thank you for the music
I put on my CD player
before going to work,
before going to school.

For the joy and exploration of jazz
for the calm of easy-listening
for the 'How long?' of blues
for the peace and perfection of classical music
for the heart of country
for the honesty of folk
for the anger of punk
for the passion of rock
for the spirit of dance
for the Soul of soul
for tunes compact and perfect as
the Lord's Prayer.

Lord of the singing spheres
thank you for the music
I put on my CD player
before going to work,
before going to school.

Neil Paynter

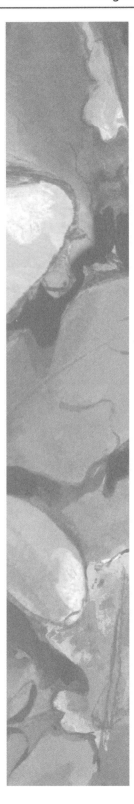

BE CHILDREN OF GOD

Do justice
Be strong
Be generous
Don't ignore those who need you
Don't damage the earth

Love mercy
Be kind
Be forgiving
Don't bear grudges
Don't withhold love

Walk humbly with your God
Be attentive
Be obedient
Don't run away from wisdom
Don't wander off the road

Love God with all that you have –
your mind, your heart, your soul,
your dreams, your tears and laughter

And love your neighbour as you love yourself
Let your children play together;
share your stories and your food

Be salt
Be light
Be leaven
Be happy

Be who you are
Be children of God

Ruth Burgess

GOD, HELP ME TO GROW

God, help me to grow
like a garden
like a song
like a tree.

Like a great tree
like one of those great, old trees
you meet sometimes and hug,
wandering lost
or enchanted
in a deep, dark forest,
in an empty field.

A great, old tree
with roots that reach down to the heart,
roots that reach down
but break through the ground around the trunk and lift
as if the earth can't contain the yearning.

A great, old tree
with arms that shelter and shade
and house such love.

A great, old tree
with breaks and wounds and scars
but dancing and clapping its hands
like a beautiful old woman at a summer wedding.

A great, old tree
still and centred
drawing on the living warm core of God
though left stripped of everything.

God, help me to grow
like a garden
like a song
like a tree.

Like one of those great, old trees
you meet sometimes

in a crowded forest
in an empty field ...

Neil Paynter

REFLECTIONS ON THE RULE OF THE IONA COMMUNITY

The five-fold Rule of the Iona Community calls Members to daily prayer and Bible reading; sharing and accounting for the use of their money; planning and accounting for the use of their time; action for justice and peace in society; meeting and accounting to each other.

On my way towards joining the Iona Community

I don't know whether I have become
more holy,
more obedient,
more prayerful.

I doubt there is
more
now
in spite of all my efforts.

But there are
more
people on my way
struggling like me and
sharing their inadequacy and their triumphs
like me.

That helps.

On daily prayer

Yes, there is more now
more habit
more desperation too:

how can I intercede for a country like Brazil
let alone the poor of this world?
I do not even know the faces
of all the Community members.

Yes, there is more reminding myself and reminding God
how needy we are
how much I lack heart.

There is more silence

spreading across this world, a garment of long suffering
before the heart of God.

On accounting for the use of money

My parents belonged to the generation that lost everything
twice in their lives.
They brought me up on generosity,
  but there was never a spare penny in our house
that could be lost
  to yet another bankrupt dictator.
I learned sharing freely
but did not learn saving.

I find it difficult to make lists of what I earn and what I need,
what I spend and what I share;
I live from hand to mouth, I'm in the red every so often,
and sometimes
I don't know whether I'm squandering my money or not.
(Shouldn't I know?)

Yes, it is useful to make lists
and tell each other
what we earn, and need and give away.

And why!

On accounting for the use of time

I have always admired those who spend their time wisely.
I envied them.
I've always over-planned and overbooked my time,
I've often done things simultaneously instead of
doing them one by one,
many women do.
I have behaved as if there were a chance
of increasing life by rolling several lives into one.

To use our time wisely means to have
accepted our mortality.
I haven't yet.
I'm still craving for life, not never-ending, but good life for all.
I want to contribute towards that goal in my time.

I want to make a difference.
I'm still in a hurry!

On committing ourselves to working for justice, peace and the integrity of creation

There was that beggar in the *Terreiro de Jesus*,
Jesus Square in Salvador de Bahia.
A young woman, haggard, thin, maybe ill or on drugs.
Aggressively demanding five *reals* for herself and the baby
and cursing me because I gave her only one.
(My last night in Brazil, I needed to keep the money for the taxi.)

Her face told me that I failed to love.
I was so concerned about my taxi that I failed
to see her humanity.

I gave the rest of the money to another beggar later.
It didn't absolve me.

I still see her face. Young. Angry.
And think.
It is not enough to write cheques.
It is not enough to go on demonstrations,
to be concerned about the system and the structures.

And all these things need to be turned around.

It is a question of relationships.
In the end I shall be asked:
Did I open my heart?
Did I make myself vulnerable?

Did I allow myself to be changed?

Meeting with each other

Yes, friends, you are now among the people
I miss.
When the going gets rough and in between
the best we ever do is
to open ourselves, to share our lives.
And not fail each other.

Yes, friends, you are now among the people I count on.

When my imagination fails me and I wonder how we can make the world
a bit more just and peaceful,
I hold on to the hope that
next time we meet we'll eat together
and pray and get bold together,
and know
God is with us, friend and lover of all.

Reinhild Traitler

ARTISTS' PRAYER

God of vision
you give us gifts of creativity.

Bless us
with courage to take new risks,
boldness to be adventurous,
and faith to know your presence.

Inspire us
to open our eyes to fresh vision.

Awaken us
to our creative possibilities,
enabling us
as empowered artists
to transform our lives,
and the life of the world. Amen

Elizabeth Baxter

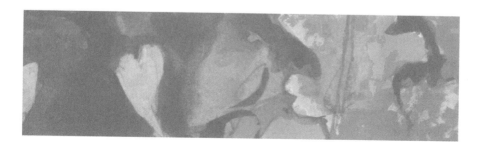

THIS IS THE LORD'S DOING

Creator God, who made the whole universe
that you might share your glory with your creatures,
we bless you that, as it was planted in space and time by love,
so is life planted in the world, age by age,
by the love of man and woman.
We thank you that we are fearfully and wonderfully made,
mysteriously wrought and brought to full stature,
changing through the years and yet the same.
We bless you that we are differently gifted,
each one precious and endowed:
This is the Lord's doing
and it is marvellous in our eyes.

Almighty God, whose Son taught us what love is,
in his living and dying for others,
we bless you that he loves us just as we are,
whatever we have done and been:
those who have wandered in some far country
or have wasted their substance in decorous living
or have done his will humbly in difficult places:
all alike unworthy, all treasured.
We bless you that he teaches us integrity in our relationships,
and gives us power to put others before ourselves,
that we might tame our desires,
and love with imagination and self-forgetfulness:
This is the Lord's doing
and it is marvellous in our eyes.

O Blessed God, whose Spirit begets a host of dancing things,
we thank you for the ecstasy of life,
the sway of bodies and the light of eyes,
the toss of hair, the touch of hands,
the grace and comeliness of manhood and womanhood;
and for the gay spirit in handicapped bodies
the quiet light in old eyes
the assertion of life where illness and hurt have left their mark.
We bless you for bodies made temples of the Holy Spirit:
This is the Lord's doing
and it is marvellous in our eyes.

Ian M Fraser

GROW IN GOD

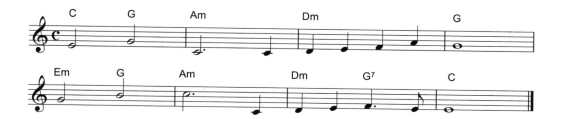

Grow in God,
be grounded in God's love.
Grow in God,
strong in your inner selves.

Grow in God,
and rooted in your faith.
Grow in God
abounding in Christ's joy.

Grow in God,
God's presence fill your life.
Grow in God,
Christ's peace within your hearts.

Carol Dixon

SEEING THE WORLD

We like our way of seeing the world, Holy One.
It is familiar to us, but it excludes other perspectives.
We prefer our way of knowing and understanding you, Holy One.
It is familiar to us, but it limits who we accept in our midst.
We find comfort in our criticism of governments and political leaders, Holy One.
It is familiar to us, but it is often followed by inaction.
Forgive our complacency.
Forgive our apathy.
Forgive our small-mindedness.
Amen

Holly Benzenhafer Redford

ANSWERS

When eternity comes
maybe God will sort it all out:

the unanswered questions
that keep us awake at night;
the undeserved suffering
that pains us;
the brokenness which,
no matter how hard we try,
we cannot mend.

Someday,
when eternity comes,
maybe God will sort it all out
but until then
we know:

love showered earth
when Jesus came,
and flows from us to others;

hope was planted in our hearts
and we wait for the harvest;

joy became our soul's companion
and yearns to walk with us;

grace was the gift
we cannot exchange;

and these are all the
answers
we have

until eternity comes.

Thom M Shuman

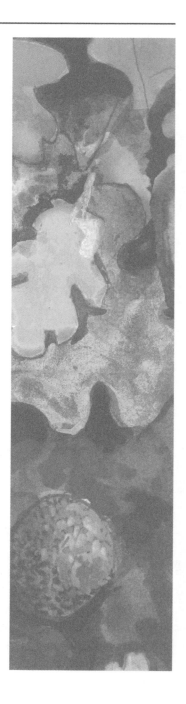

THE MINISTRY OF GOD'S PEOPLE

(Tune: Water of Tyne)

This day, as we gather, we celebrate here
the service of all who are called on to share
in the task of God's ministry, serving this place;
we rejoice that God fills those he calls with his grace.

As Peter and Andrew first heard Jesus' call,
then Dorcas and Lydia who worked beside Paul,
and Francis and Clare, helping others to see
that together we all share in Christ's ministry.

We give of ourselves to God in all we do,
as we listen, and share hospitality too;
to pray and to preach some are chosen and sent,
so our work and our worship become sacrament.

To God, our Creator, we now dedicate
our lives, our worship, and here consecrate
our work for God's kingdom, and offering all
in the strength of the Spirit, we respond to Christ's call

Carol Dixon

LOOK AFTER ME

Dear God,
please look after me
and make me do stuff right.

Gemma, aged 8

THERE ARE DAYS

There are days
when I go through three pens
crafting my to-do list.
From the moment
the alarm shoves me
out of bed
until my pillow
rocks me to sleep,
I am going and doing and running,
cleaning and washing and shopping,
cooking and serving and clearing.

And then
Jesus comes in the door,
sits me down at the table,
pours me a cup of tea, saying,
'Be still. Shush. Listen. Learn.'

There are days
when I am all ears,
pondering words,
listening to scholars whisper,
being lullabied by commentators,
sitting and reflecting and doing nothing,
silent and hushed and thinking.

And then Amos interrupts
my alone time,
saying,
'You wanna learn something?
Come, sit at the feet of the poor;
they'll teach you more about
faith and hope and love and life,
compassion and grace and gentleness
than you'll ever need.'

There are days ...

Thom M Shuman

THE PURPLE WHEELIE BIN

We give thanks for the purple wheelie bin,
receptacle of all our rubbish,
carrier-away of our cast-offs, unused goods,
undigested foodstuffs, nappies, wrappers,
broken electrical items and all the discarded clutter
of our cupboards and our lives.

A blessing on those who make it their work
to collect these bins together
and pour their contents into a waiting lorry,
labouring through soaking rain and stinking heat on behalf of
    the rest of us wasteful citizens.

A blessing on those who wheel out the bins for their forgetful or frail neighbours,
and wheel them in again afterwards.

A blessing on those who brighten up their wheelie bins
    by painting on them pictures of flowers,
favourite TV characters or cartoonish self-portraits.

We give thanks for the purple wheelie bin,
receptacle of all our rubbish.

Give us patience with those who use our wheelie bins as playthings:
climbing on them,
racing down the road in them like plastic chariots,
setting them on fire.

Give us strength to push our full and heavy bins to the roadside
when we are feeling feeble on bin collection morning.

Keep us calm if, in a moment of panic,
we should think our bin has gone,
wheeled away up the road or into oblivion.

Help us to forgive those who, years ago now,
decided without asking us
that our bins should be purple.

Help us to recycle,
and bless those who want to help us to recycle more.

Help us to use less packaging,

and bless those who want to sell us
things with less packaging on them.

Give us grace to care about our waste
and the way it affects our city's space.

We give thanks for the purple wheelie bin,
receptacle of all our rubbish. Amen

John Davies

RESPONDING TO GOD

God has the right to ask daft things of people and expect them to respond. For God is God.

I have seen it high in the Italian mountains where a centre, mainly for youth, was being built in about as awkward a place to reach as you could think of. Tullio Vinay was there alone. The money had run out at that point. Work had stopped. Tullio held out his arms to us and said, 'How heavy are empty hands!' He had gone there because he was told to. There was no guarantee that he had done the right thing. I still receive in the post the annual programme of that flourishing centre.

George MacLeod was disturbed at a way of living which threw people out of employment and had so little justice in it. He looked for political and economic redress. So he went to the isle of Iona, which in Columba's time was relatively easily accessed compared with central Scotland because the sea was a highway. But Iona had by then become a tiny spot on the fringes of Europe, not easily reached. He gathered a team of craftsmen and probationer ministers to rehabilitate the ruined outbuildings of the Abbey. The Second World War was one of many stumbling blocks. He was once found in tears in the Abbey because the whole project seemed to be a wild goose chase. He went to Iona because he was told to. The Iona Community is now a force in the World Church.

The genealogy of Matthew, which gives the build-up through history to the coming of Jesus Christ, starts with Abraham. He was not picked on by God because he was righteous. He was picked on because God fingered him. He became righteous and an example for succeeding generations because he responded. Responded to what? To the command: 'Go from your country and your kindred and your father's house to the land that I will show you.' Any long-distance lorry driver would think a company off its head which gave the order: 'Start off and keep going. I'll tell you when you reach the place.'

Wives of patriarchs in early Bible stories had difficulty bringing forth children. Abraham's wife, Sarah, was no exception. A child by her maidservant turned out to be no substitute. Sarah, when past childbearing age, conceived and gave birth to Isaac. When the lad was grown what did God do? Something inconceivably daft. God had promised that Abraham would be father of a great nation in whom all families of the earth would be blessed. The thin line of promise depended on lineage through Isaac – and God asked Abraham to sacrifice his beloved son! It did not add up. But Abraham obeyed. Sarah would have torn his hair out and shut Isaac away had she known. But clearly he did not tell her. A ram caught in a thicket saved the situation. In later history, God's beloved Son, on whom the exodus for humanity from every form of slavery depended (Luke 9:31), would be put to death. That made no sense – until the resurrection took place and that death was seen to be fruitful for all life. Abraham's obedience was a sign of hope.

How difficult it is at times to sort out daftnesses which are daft and God's daftnesses which are creative and have saving power. Yet, while there are great saints who get prominence, who undertake actions which forward God's Kingdom of justice and peace, the biblical understanding includes people who are not prominent. All kinds of people respond to God, following callings which may seem humdrum, unimportant. The idea of vocation became limited in the Middle Ages. The word came to be used solely for the call to the religious (monastic) life. But the New Testament understanding embraces all those who respond to God. In 1 Corinthians 11:26, Paul makes this clear: *'Consider your own calling, brothers and sisters; not many of you were wise by human standards, not many were powerful, not many were of noble birth. But God chose what is foolish in the world to shame the wise; God chose what is weak in the world to shame the strong; God chose what is low and despised in the world – things that are not, to reduce to nothing things that are, so that no one might boast in the presence of God.'* Vocation is a call to availability. The availability is to do whatever is wanted, whatever one's job – for me it meant breaking away from the usual parish assignment, to work with labouring gangs in industry. For those of us who are ordained, the calling is simply to availability, not to a particular status. We all have to do whatever is wanted by God.

My Uncle Bill was a carter. He carted stones for roads and barley for the local distillery. When people spoke about him they inevitably described him as 'far ben', i.e. specially close to God. Was my vocation in ordained ministry any more important than that of my carter uncle?

The bright young lass in the Dunfermline fish shop at which we were customers, when we served Rosyth, took the chance, when there was no queue, to say to me, 'It must be great to have a job like yours – doing good all day, every day.' I replied, 'Your cheerful service all day and every day to people who come into this shop may count for more than anything I ever did in my life.' She was mystified and, at the same time, a bit encouraged.

People respond to God in all types of work which brings life safely forward from one day to another, often without knowing that they are making a response through their working life. In the book of Ecclesiasticus, in chapters 37 and 39, there is appreciation of the contribution of good advisors and medical doctors and scholars. In Chapter 38 the writer focuses on jobs which seem less important. Who is it who maintain the fabric of the world, day after day? He highlights the work of the ploughman, the blacksmith, the potter. But are they responding to God by doing their work well? The writer answers: 'Their daily work is their prayer.'

Those of us who are ordained have particular and important gifts to bring, but we must not exaggerate their importance. The ministry or priesthood which accompanies that of Jesus Christ's High Priesthood is committed to the whole people of God. It is their response which is decisive.

Ian M Fraser

ALWAYS KNEW

I always knew there was no God in the sky.
I always knew Jesus's dad didn't exist.
I could see that God was made in man's image,
but beyond that was fog; was sightlessness.
I kept these views to myself, I'm no fool.
The 'I'm right, so you're wrong brigade' often kill.
Another's delusions is a sorry reason for dying.
All delusions need the nutrient of darkness
and light's terrifying when you're shackled in shadow.

So after many years of care and research
I stated (to myself) with confidence,
'I am an unconditional atheist!'
Immediately I knew this was untrue.

There was still that which cannot be articulated,
a knowledge which cannot be written of,
which has joy as a mark;
mayhap approached through a door of silence,
tethered in the very second you read this word.
When I sensed this, I smiled, and smiled, and smiled.
(But relax ... If you don't believe me I won't kill you,
I'm not that scared, plus I might be wrong.)

Stuart Barrie

OPEN HANDS

Open hands;
to receive
to offer,
not clinging
or grasping,
accepting
and passing on.

Open hands;
not controlling
but unique
and vulnerable,
marked with life.

Open hands;
holding past
and present
and future
together,
with love
with hope.

Julia Brown

WEAVER

O Weaver,
shuttling the thread of glory
through the pattern of our days.
Come, bed us down
into the cloth of earth and heaven.
Come clothe us with joy.

Ruth Burgess

BRIGHT AND CHEERFUL

Dear God,
thank you for all the wonderful things in the world.
Help us to be bright and cheerful. Amen

Christopher, aged 7

GOD IS GREAT

Life is great
full of glad surprises;
life is tough –
stony paths we've trod!
What makes sense
each day sun arises:
God.

God holds back
venturing matures us;
God steps in
giving strength to cope:
God's wise love
gives the whole creation
hope.

God transforms
through the gifts we're given;
leagued with him
we make the world anew:

justice, love mark
a way of life that's
true.

Roll up sleeves
use each life entrusted,
take sure hold
of transforming power:
work with God
venturing to meet this
hour.

Ian M Fraser

ALL THOSE FACES

All those faces, God the Lord!
Familiar ones in the house,
strange ones in the street,
each one made in your likeness
yet none the mirror of another;
family resemblances, yes, even look-alikes,
but over millions of years, no duplicates.
What a craftsman you are
creating different identities in such short space!
It is as if you were telling us
that each one of us is special
and loved as if there were no one else. Alleluia! Amen

Ian M Fraser

I HOPE

Dear God,
I hope when I go to the doctors tonight,
I hope he doesn't put a needle in it.

Marie, aged 7

GRANDMA'S BLESSING

Health in the springtime of your life.
The hue of briar rose upon your cheek.
Strong and supple limbs to stride through
life and embrace all that it will offer.
Deep peace in your soul.
The courage of lions in your heart.

Love to fall like April rain upon your hurts.
Love to shine like summer sun on your joys.
Love to gold balm your sorrows
when September sunsets come.
Love in all your winter griefs
till new life wakes again.

Norah Hanson

MY FAMILY

Dear God,
I hope you are looking after my family in heaven.
I would love to see my granddad and my nana again.

Tony, aged 8

FATHER, SON AND HOLY SPIRIT

Father, Son and Holy Spirit, accept our thanks
for those who honour you without knowing it:
who collaborate with you in upholding the creation –
building and repairing houses and roads,
driving road, rail and air transport, serving in shops and offices,
tending animals and crops, rearing children,
sustaining the fabric of the world for one more day at a time;
and for those who hearten others by the cheerful way they face up to life,
lightening loads, seeing the funny side, ready with sympathy;
who, at the last, may be taken aback to hear Christ's 'Well done',
for they had not realised that what was done for others was done for him.
Amen

Ian M Fraser

ALL HALLOWS'

WINDOW BOX IN AUTUMN

Purple pansies shivering in a pot,
the early sunlight on their smiling faces
defying the frosty earth;
velvet petals, cold to the touch,
silky soft, still showing signs of summer.

Memories of warmer days in Italy and France:
red-barned farm in the Suisse Normande,
chattering chickens and voluble farm wives,
excited dogs and solid farmers
in blue overalls, leisurely leaning
across the fence for an afternoon smoke:
'B'jour m'seur, m'dame,'
with the quiet courtesy of the country kind;

and a solitary cross in pitted stone –
purple pansies at its foot –
remembrance of young men lost
in battles long forgotten.

Carol Dixon

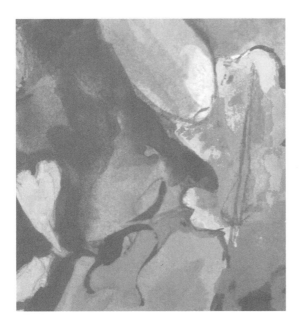

AND STILL YOU TARRY

Early closing
for autumn evenings,
escorting all souls
into November.
Gunpowder lingers
trapped in the mist,
the plangent 'Last Post' dies away.

And still, leaves, you tarry

holding tenaciously to your greenness
refusing to let go.

And then with a gasp
you open the paintbox
spilling the glory ...

Burnt sienna, burnt ochre,
yellow ochre, liquid amber,
vermillion, scarlet and crimson lake
vie with each other,
trembling with joy.

Late in the Suffolk afternoon
an aubergine sky threatens rain.
Against the darkness
sun-shafts catch the leaves alight
with incandescent mastery.
Here and there a lacy skeleton
dances on the gusty horizon
as if glad to be done with it all.

Next morning
skylarks
blithely surrender to the buffeting storm.

Each to its season
and I
must now wait for Advent.

Rosie Watson

CRAB APPLES

Crab apples.
Not big peach and golden ones you'd choose for making jelly,
or admire hanging from a neighbour's John Downie,
but through the kitchen window panes,
festooned in clusters small and green,
among the dark well-veined leaves
of the straggling unpruned tree,
a crop of little fruits you see.
They're in need of much attention,
a few will drop and rot,
but some will still remain
through November's wind and rain.
Then along bare branches,
tinged with silver frost,
outshine the Christmas baubles,
to enjoy a New Year gaudy.

Don't be deceived by crabby apples
or by many crabby-looking masks
crowded behind doors marked E.M.I.
They too can catch the winter sunshine,
reflect some fun,
defy the coldest blast.
All saints, all souls, at last!

Liz Gregory-Smith

Notes: *E.M.I. – elderly mentally ill;*
          gaudy – a party or celebration

ALL HALLOWS

All Hallows
All Saints
All Souls
All holy

Weekly we say the words,
'We look for the
resurrection of the dead

and the life
of the world to come.'*

Those who have died
are part of us.
We name them,
we tell their stories.

The love they had for us
and we for them
is not dead
is not forgotten.

They may be alive
in another world
but we cannot
know that.

And when we die
we do not know
what will happen
to us.

We do not know
what life there is to come.

All living
All looking
All dying
All mystery

All the journey

Give me what I can grasp
and your love to keep me holy,
I will walk with you, God.

Ruth Burgess

* *The Nicene Creed*

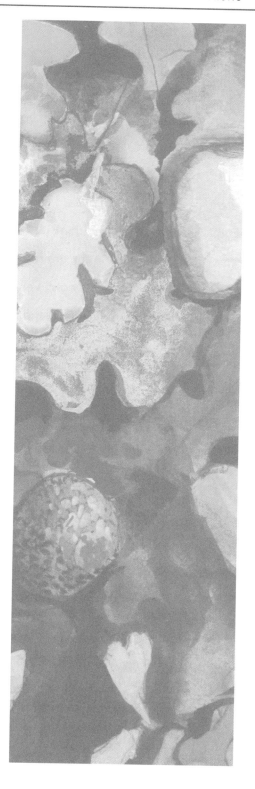

TRICK OR TREAT

(A two-act play for Hallowe'en)

Act I

A conversation at the gate of heaven between Jesus and Peter.

Peter: Eh, Jesus!

Jesus: Yes, Peter.

Peter: Have you ever heard of a place called Scotland?

Jesus: Maybe I have, I think it's away beyond Jerusalem, Judaea and Samaria.

Peter: Perhaps it's in the uttermost parts of the earth.

Jesus: You're probably right, Peter. That's where it will be. Why did you ask me?

Peter: Funny people in Scotland.

Jesus: There are funny people everywhere, Peter, even in Jerusalem. What's so funny about Scotland?

Peter: Well, my brother Andrew is the patron saint there.

Jesus: I thought he was the patron saint of Romania.

Peter: He's that also. They keep him pretty busy you know. But he was telling me about Scotland, how gangs of wee boys and girls go roaming around the streets knocking on people's doors and shouting: 'Trick or treat?!'

Jesus: Is that what they do on St Andrew's Night?

Peter: No. They do it on Hallowe'en.

Jesus: Hallow what?

Peter: Hallowe'en. It's the night before All Saints' Day, on November 1st. 'Hallow' – it's a different kind of language from Hebrew. They write it from left to right.

Jesus: That's amazing! Front to back!

Peter: Yes. It's a language called English. 'Hallow' is an old English word, like they spoke when that chap Henry was around, you know 'the Eighth', the one who started a new branch of your Church. Well, in those days 'hallow' meant 'holy', like in the prayer you gave us once. You remember: 'Hallowed be Thy name.'

Jesus:	Oh yes, I remember, they say it every day, or at least every Sunday in church. But what's all this got to do with All Saints' Day?
Peter:	Well, hallow means holy and holy is what saints are.
Jesus:	Ah, now I get it. So it's a holy night before All Saints' Day.
Peter:	That's it. You got it.
Jesus:	But what's that to do with this trick or treat business?
Peter:	I'm not sure, but I'll go down there and find out.

Act II

Somewhere in Argyll, outside a cottage door. Peter knocks on the door.

Alasdair:	Well, well – and who are you, knocking at this time of night?
Peter:	My name's Peter. Can I come in?
Alasdair:	Yes, come away in ... Can we offer you some Highland hospitality? A wee dram perhaps?
Peter:	And what might that be?
Alasdair:	Some whisky. It's a drink.
Peter:	No thank you, I only drink wine. What I want to ask you is whether you know anything about Hallowe'en?
Alasdair:	I know it's on 31st October but I don't know that much about it. My sister will know. She's a dab hand at all that kind of thing, very religious you know. *(Shouting)* Are you there, Morag? *(Enter Morag)* There you are now. Can you tell this gentleman about Hallowe'en?
Morag:	And what would you be wanting to know?
Peter:	My brother, who is very fond of Scotland, has told me about something called 'trick or treat?' and my Master and I are curious to know more about it. So I've come to find out.
Morag:	Well, it's a long story but I'll keep it short. For our Celtic ancestors the 31st October was the time when they returned with their herds from the sheilings in the high mountain pastures. The 1st November was the beginning of the New Year when land tenures and other things were renewed. They also thought it was the time when the souls of the dead were supposed to revisit their homes, and there was a lot of nonsense about ghosts and

witches, hobgoblins, fairies and demons roaming around. They used to light huge bonfires to frighten away evil spirits. It was before people heard about Jesus.

Peter: So you know about Jesus?

Alasdair: Do you?

Peter: Just a bit. He is my Lord and Master.

Morag: Well, that's very good. Far too few people know about Jesus these days. He's the one who put the evil spirits in their place and whom they call the Son of God. Thus the ancient customs have now become child's play, like trick or treat.

Peter: Ah, trick or treat, that's what Andrew was on about. How does it work?

Morag: Well, it's about good and evil. Long ago Moses gave people a choice. He told them: 'See, I have set before you this day life and good, death and evil. Choose life.' We still have that choice between the trickery of evil and the reward that goodness brings. It's a case of trick or treat.

Alasdair: If you're wise you'll ask for a treat. They might sing you a wee song or something. Otherwise it might be something nasty!

Morag: It's all a bit of fun to remind us of serious things as we prepare for All Saints' Day and give thanks for those who, in the power of Jesus, have overcome evil with good. We call them the saints in heaven. Some are quite famous like Peter, the real Peter I mean, and others are our own loved ones who have gone before us and for whom we give thanks on All Saints' Day. They're all around us, especially in our worship.

Alasdair: How would you like to come to our Hallowe'en party?

Peter: Thanks so much, but I've got to get back now. I hope you have a heavenly party! Goodbye.

Murdoch MacKenzie

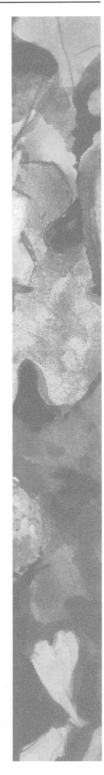

A SERVICE FOR SAMHAIN FROM IONA ABBEY

Introduction

Leader: As the Wheel of the Year turns towards winter, the nights get longer. The endless summer evenings are far behind us now, and darkness has come in their place. Winds howl and leaves fall. And, on this island, visitors dwindle, hotels close, the birds depart for warmer climes, and many of us prepare to depart as well. The world rests, and we are invited to rest with it.

Opening responses

Let the darkness of night surround us,
let light and warmth gather us
and let God's people say Amen.
AMEN

Let the tools be stored away,
let the work be over and done
and let God's people say Amen.
AMEN

Let the winds blow wild around us,
but let hearts be glad and minds be calm
and let God's people say Amen.
AMEN [1]

Leader: Tonight is Samhain, traditionally the start of the dark half of the year. Samhain means 'summer's end', and is the Gaelic word for the month of November. In Christian tradition, tonight is the eve of All Hallows' Day, All Hallows' Even, from where we get the word Hallowe'en.

In this time, in this country, this night means different things to different people.

Reader 1: A time to honour ancestors and remember loved ones who have died.

Reader 2: A night when the veil between the worlds grows thin.

Reader 3: A ritual of reversal, when trick or treating allows children to wreak havoc on grown-ups.

Reader 4: A night of fire and ritual.

Reader 5: An excuse to dress up and party, to wear strange clothes and be someone or something entirely different.

Reader 6:   A time to mark the changing of the seasons and prepare for the coming winter.

Blessings of the dark

Leader: Tonight, we honour the passing of the summer and welcome the autumn, rejoicing in the Light of Christ, who is always with us through the dark nights of winter and the dark nights of our lives.

Reader 1:   It is only in the dark that we can see the stars.

Reader 2:   Sometimes, it is only when we cannot see that we begin to hear.

Reader 3:   In darkness we have the freedom not to be seen, to withdraw, to encounter God and our deepest selves.

Reader 4:   In darkness we are encouraged to cease our outward explorations, to turn our hearts to home and to those with whom we share it.

Reader 5:   The dark dissolves our bright illusions of independence, and reminds us to reach out and feel God's hand in ours.

Reader 6:   In darkness, the world rests. As the trees shed their leaves, we can shed what we no longer need to carry. And as the rotting leaves nourish the germinating seeds, we can allow God to nourish our dreams until they are ready to grow into action.

Leader: In gratitude for the gifts of darkness, we sing 'Thank You for the Night':

                Song: 'Thank You for the Night' (John L. Bell and Graham Maule, from *Iona Abbey Music Book*, Wild Goose Publications)

Liturgy of Light

Leader: Darkness can be frightening. Shadows make the familiar unfamiliar, and fear conjures monsters that seem to lurk just out of sight. But rather than carving fierce pumpkin faces to scare away those of whom we are afraid, Christ invites us to put our trust in him and walk in his light.

Reader 1:   Often, it is hard to see the way ahead. O God, as we stumble through life, trying to work things out, teach us to trust your guiding hand.

Reader 2:   *(lights candle)* May a light shine in the darkness of our confusion.

Reader 3:   Sometimes, we lose our way in the dark. O God, when we are in pain, whether it is the pain of loneliness, bereavement, addiction, illness, broken relationships or any other trials, open our hearts to receive your comfort.

Reader 4:   *(lights candle)* May a light shine in the darkness of our pain.

Reader 5:   At all times, O God, you are with us.
There is nowhere that you are not present.
Search us, O God, and know our minds and hearts,
test us and discover our thoughts.
Find out if there is any evil in us,
and guide us in ways that are everlasting.

Reader 6:   *(lights candle)* May a light shine in the darkness of our souls.

(Pause)

Leader: O God, darkness is not dark for you,
for you the night is as bright as the day.
Darkness and light are the same to you.

AND MAY YOU KINDLE WITHIN US A FLAME THAT NEVER DIES.

Leader: As we sing the next song, we will pass the flame between us, an external symbol of the fires we are inviting God to light within us.

Chant : 'Dans Nos Obscurités' (Taizé)

Closing blessing

Through the turning of the seasons
BLESS US WITH WILDNESS AND WONDER

Through our nights and our days
BLESS US WITH ADVENTURE AND COURAGE

Through the journeys of our lives
BLESS US WITH HEALING AND HOPE

And through your blessings may we know your joy within us:
Star-maker,
Light of the world,
Fire of holiness,
LOVE WITHOUT END. AMEN [2]

Carole Birley and Philippa Pearson

Notes

1. Opening responses © The Iona Community, from The Iona Abbey Worship Book, *Wild Goose Publications, 2001 www.ionabooks.com*

2. Closing blessing © Ruth Burgess

A candle is needed for each person participating in this liturgy.

GOING

THE TIME THAT IS YOURS

God bless to you the time that is yours.
God bless to you the time that is now.
God bless to you the time that he has given.
God bless to you each day,
each hour,
each passing moment,
that you may pass it in his presence
and find him in it.
Amen

David Hamflett

OUR TRUE BEGINNING

The blessing of God
the mother and father
of the created universe,

the blessing of Jesus
the brother and sister
of all humankind,

the blessing of the Holy Spirit
who dances like a dervish
through all our lives and experiences,

enfold us
as we continue our journey
to the ending,
which will be our true beginning.

Stanley Baxter

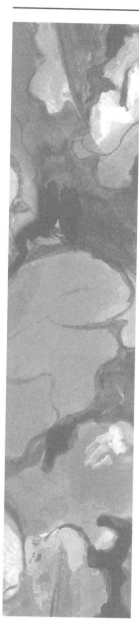

A HEBRIDEAN BLESSING

May the song of the lark
fill your heart with joy,
the gentle Iona breeze caress you
and give you deep peace.
May all your days be filled
with the delight of puffins,
and may the outpourings of the Holy Spirit
in your life
be as magnificent as Fingal's cave.

Heather Olsen

A STILL CENTRE

Be still
and listen to the day,
touch the breeze
with the quiet in your soul.

Let the turning turbulence
of the hurly-burly rushing,
the busy dizzy people,
pass you by.

God bless you
with a quiet whisper,
which in all the day's doing
keeps a calm silent centre
in your being.

Chris Polhill

SEND US OUT

Send us out
Send us out to seek wisdom
SEND US OUT IN PEACE

Send us out
Send us out to do justice
SEND US OUT IN HOPE

Send us out
Send us out to be loving
SEND US OUT IN JOY

Ruth Burgess

GO OUT INTO THE WORLD

Go out into the world to meet people

and find them no longer strangers
but fellow travellers;

no longer aliens to be avoided
but family to be welcomed;

no longer enemies to be feared
but friends to be enjoyed.

Go out into the world to meet God's people!

Pat Bennett

IN THE MIDST OF THE STORM

Let us go out,
trusting in the love, faithfulness and power of Jesus.
May we know his peace
even in the midst of the storm.
And the blessing of God,
Saviour, Lord and Friend,
be upon us now
and for evermore. Amen

Simon Taylor

GO NOW

Go now
Go with God's blessing
Go in justice and love.

Go now
Go and love your neighbour
Go and respect the earth.

Go now
Go and befriend strangers
Go and make peace.

Go now
It is time
Go and walk with God.

Ruth Burgess

BENEDICTION

May all your hopes be sustained
between the wings of seagulls,
and may your fears, before they start,
be taloned fast by eagles.

May curling salmon leap the falls
on the river of your strife,
and pine trees crack with age
in the forests of your life.

May speckled fawns raise their heads
beneath your vaulted blue,
and may the God of frost and stars
be evermore with you.

Robert Davidson

SOURCES AND ACKNOWLEDGEMENTS

'One day' – first published in *The Pattern of Our Days*, Wild Goose Publications, 1996 www.ionabooks.com

'A Thessalonian rap' – by Ruth Burgess, first published by CTBI, 2007 © Ruth Burgess.

'Wholly God' – by Ruth Harvey, first published in *Pushing the Boat Out: New Poetry*, Kathy Galloway (ed.), Wild Goose Publications, 1995 www.ionabooks.com

'Stone angel' – by Ruth Burgess, originally published in *At Ground Level*, Ruth Burgess, Wild Goose Publications (out of print).

'The fruits of loving' – by Scott Blythe, first published in *Coracle*, the magazine of the Iona Community www.iona.org.uk

'Global garden' – by Pete Anderson, first published in *Coracle*, the magazine of the Iona Community www.iona.org.uk

'Benediction' – by Robert Davidson, first published in *Coracle*, the magazine of the Iona Community www.iona.org.uk

'No shoes' – by Kirsty Thomas, first published on a poster to celebrate the installation of 'The Angel of the North', a sculpture in Gateshead. Poster published by Northern Arts.

'Two wings' – by Adam Pearson, first published on a poster to celebrate the installation of 'The Angel of the North', a sculpture in Gateshead. Poster published by Northern Arts.

CONTRIBUTORS

Rowena Aberdeen recently spent three years on Iona as the MacLeod Centre Warden and is now enjoying the daily challenge of finding ways to live community in new places and different contexts.

Alison Adam is a member of the Iona Community. She leads workshops on worship and song.

Sofia Adrian is a former volunteer at Iona and Camas. At the moment she is doing teacher training in biology and science.

Pete Anderson is a former member of the Iona Community's resident group on Iona.

Francine Asonibare left Britain for Nigeria as a child and spent 20 years living and working there. After her return, she began to write poetry again, and in particular sacred poetry.

Stuart Barrie – 'Glasgow-born and trained engineer now domiciled in the arctic wastes of East Kilbride. Retired mountaineer, present poet, real purpose of life still unknown.'

Elizabeth Baxter and Stanley Baxter are Anglican Priests and Executive Directors of Holy Rood House Centre for Health and Pastoral Care and The Centre for the Study of Theology and Health, Thirsk, North Yorkshire. 'We enjoy supporting people on their spiritual and therapeutic journeys and our four children and six grandchildren keep us grounded, challenge us and bring us delight!'

Pat Bennett is an associate member of the Iona Community who has been writing assorted liturgical material since her first stay on Iona in 1996. She is currently working on a PhD linking theology and neuroscience and exploring the connection between relationality and health.

Holly Benzenhafer Redford is a minister affiliated with Alliance of Baptists and holds a Master of Divinity, specialising in Spirituality, from Boston University School of Theology. A contemplative, liturgist, poet and scholar, she continues to explore the interweaving of spiritual practice with intentional community.

Jan Berry is a minister in the United Reformed Church who teaches practical theology at Luther King House in Manchester. She has published material for worship in various anthologies, and lives with her partner, two cats and a dog.

Carole Birley spent three months as a volunteer staff member of the Iona Community in autumn 2008. She now works on environmental issues for the Diocese of Bradford.

Scott Blythe is a member of the Iona Community and an Interim Pastor within the Presbyterian Church of USA. His interests range from poetry to movies, walking to swimming, philosophy to politics and all that seeks to unite faith and action in today's fragmented world.

Cally Booker lives in Dundee and worships at St Paul's Cathedral. She is a research student, a weaver, a bit absent-minded and passionate about cheeses.

Ruth Bowen lives and works in the Orkney Islands. Her interests are prayer, needlecraft, gardening and people.

Julia Brown works in Durham where she lives with her husband and three children. She loves the sense of freedom she feels when writing poetry.

Nick Burden is an associate of the Iona Community. He lives in Newcastle upon Tyne and worships at St Gabriel's Church, Heaton.

Ruth Burgess is a writer and an editor, currently house-hunting in Dunblane. She enjoys fireworks, growing vegetables and walking in woods and along the beach. She is a member of the Iona Community.

Beryl Chatfield is a retired teacher and United Reformed Church Minister. She is interested in people, world development and interfaith dialogue.

David J.M. Coleman is a URC minister in Brighton, digital artist, occasional writer and broadcaster, married to Zam Walker, and father to Taliesin and Melangell. He is a member of the Iona Community.

Ian Cowie was born in an impoverished upper-class family, fought in the Second World War, was invalided out, and became a minister. He served in three working-class parishes before becoming full-time leader of the Christian Fellowship of Healing. He joined the Iona Community in 1945 and remained passionately committed to the project until his death in 2005.

Katrina Crosby is a former resident staff member now located on the isle of Mull, where she works part-time at Ardalanish, Isle of Mull Weavers and Organic Farm.

Robert Davidson is a long-time friend of the Iona Community. He is also the founder of Sandstone Press.

John Davies is a member of the Iona Community.

Lisa Debney lives in Ilkley with husband, Peter, and their four children. She has an MA (Dist) in Arts Education and works freelance as a writer and workshop leader.

Simon de Voil is a singer-songwriter and former resident of the MacLeod Centre. He is currently trying his hand at wooden boat building with the hope of exploring work and worship through this declining artisan trade.

Judy Dinnen has worn many hats – wife, teacher, mother, social worker, poet and now Priest and grandmother too. She is also an associate of the Iona Community and a lover of the island, the waves, rocks and the colours in the sky. These make a wonderful contrast to the green hills, apple trees and distant mountains of the Herefordshire countryside where she lives.

Carol Dixon was born in Alnwick, Northumberland and is a lay preacher in the United Reformed Church. Her hymns have been published in All Year Round, Songs for the New Millennium, Worship Live, and the Church of Scotland Hymnbook. Carol is a wife and mother with a daughter and twin sons, and enjoys spending time with her grandchildren.

Leith Fisher was a Church of Scotland minister, a hymn writer and the author of *Will You Follow Me?: Exploring the Gospel of Mark*, and *The Widening Road – from Bethlehem to Emmaus: Exploring the Gospel of Luke* (Scottish Christian Press). He was a member of the Iona Community for over forty years.

Ian Fraser is a member of the Iona Community and the author of about twenty books. His most recent is *The Way Ahead: Grown-up Christians* (Wild Goose Publications) www.ionabooks.com. Throughout his life Ian has travelled the globe, alone and with his wife, Margaret, visiting basic Christian communities.

Brian Ford – 'I was a sixth-form college biology teacher. I thought I would have lots of time to write poetry when I retired; I was wrong.'

Alma Fritchley is a tax collector and therefore one of the original sinners. She lives in Manchester with her partner, a dog and two cats.

Kathy Galloway is the current Leader of the Iona Community.

Tom Gordon is a writer and storyteller, and has been chaplain at the Marie Curie Hospice in Edinburgh since 1994. He is the author of *A Need for Living* and *New Journeys Now Begin* (Wild Goose Publications), and is a regular contributor to Wild Goose anthologies.

Alison Gray is from Glasgow but lives in Tokyo. She writes, promotes fair trade and facilitates a feminist theology discussion group.

Julie Greenan – 'I live in Saltaire, West Yorkshire. I love laughing, cycling and the Scottish islands; I'm quite impatient.'

Liz Gregory-Smith is married with two adult sons. She enjoys writing, alongside her responsibilities as a reader in the local Anglican village church. She has also been able to do some teaching in Rwanda during 2008 and hopefully 2009.

David Hamflett is a Methodist minister and a friend of the Iona Community, working in the north of England, and has a special interest in compiling and composing liturgies. He sings traditional folk songs and plays the guitar and the bodhrán.

Sheila Hamil is a priest in the Church of England, retired from parish work in the North-East of England, but still keen to do outreach work and evangelism projects wherever God leads. She is also a Christian singer-songwriter, and a drama and assembly scriptwriter. Much of her work can be obtained through her website: www.sheilahamil.co.uk

Mary Hanrahan – 'I am married with three grown-up children, and teach in a local primary school. I am an active member of St Paul the Apostle RC Church in Shettleston.'

Margaret Harvey is a founder member of the Coleg y Groes Community and helps to run the Coleg y Groes Retreat House in Corwen, North Wales (www.colegygroes. co.uk). She is a native of Wales and a Church in Wales priest.

Ruth Harvey is a Congregational Facilitator for the Church of Scotland. She lives in Penrith with Nick, Maeve, Freya and Sophie.

David Hawkey – 'Fingerprints, footprints and fire experiences have revealed God's intimate, engaged and vulnerable loving through an exciting life's journey. Turning the world's values upside down has never been more challenging than now!'

Annie Heppenstall is exploring spirituality in relation to the natural world through art and writing and has two books in print with Wild Goose Publications: *Reclaiming the Sealskin* and *Wild Goose Chase*. She is married, with one son, and has recently moved to Birmingham.

Penelope Hewlett lives and works in Birmingham, with husband and three of four children still at home. She scribbles poetry around the edges of life, sometimes during sermons, then inflicts them on her family.

Judith Jessop is a Methodist minister currently working in Sheffield, a single parent caring for her two teenage children, and an associate member of the Iona Community. She is a fairtrader and is always hoping to be more involved in justice and peace issues.

Karen Jobson is a Presbyter in the British Methodist Church and Free Church Chaplain at the University of Portsmouth.

David Lemmon is a retired youth worker and youth work trainer, living in Beckenham, Kent. He is a Methodist Local Preacher and a friend of the Iona Community.

Kareen Lowther lives in Walsall in the West Midlands where she is a part-time Team

Vicar in the Bloxwich Parish. She likes singing and being with people and using creative ways to involve people in church services.

Murdoch MacKenzie is a member of the Community, was born in Glasgow, has worked in India and in England and now lives in Argyll. Most of his ministry has been in ecumenical work, latterly as research assistant at Bossey in Switzerland.

June McAllister, who lives in rural Galway, is a member of the Iona Community, and combines an eremitic life with the Community's commitment to justice and peace.

Carolyn Morris is an ex-teacher from Berkshire. She now creates her own original books and enjoys all things papery!

Heather Olsen – 'I am a retired nurse and a former elder of the United Reformed Church in St Albans. I have a two-year-old granddaughter and enjoy watercolour painting, walking, hand-chime ringing and badminton.

Mary Palmer has an MA in creative writing; she performs poetry and runs workshops in a wide variety of venues. Her first book Iona, a poetic novella, was published last year: see www.awenpublications.co.uk

Neil Paynter is working on a book on the spirituality of rock 'n' roll. His newest book is *Down to Earth* (Wild Goose Publications) www.ionabooks.com. He is an associate of the Iona Community, Editor with Wild Goose Publications and Editor of *Coracle*, the magazine of the Iona Community.

Philippa Pearson was brought up in the Anglican tradition and now identifies herself as a Celtic Christian. She graduated from Hull University in 2006 with First Class Honours in Sociology and Social Anthropology, and still lives in Hull where she sings and plays in two heavy metal bands.

Jan Sutch Pickard is a writer and storyteller living on Mull, helping to lead worship in local churches.

Chris Polhill is a member of the Iona Community. She is the author of *A Pilgrim's Guide to Iona Abbey* and co-author of *Eggs and Ashes: Practical & Liturgical Resources for Lent and Holy Week* (Wild Goose Publications). She is a priest in the Church of England.

Anikó Schütz recently moved to Edinburgh and enjoys creativity, music, nature and acrobatics. She is an associate member of the Iona Community and was part of the resident group on Iona from 2007–08.

Penny Seabrook is Associate Vicar at All Saints Fulham and a regular visitor to Iona.

Annie Sharples – 'Hello there, I am 10 years, nearly 11. I lived on Iona for 3 years and didn't want to leave. I also like reading *The Beano*.

Mary Sharples – 'Hi, age 9 years, lived on Iona for 3 years, live in Wrexham now. My favourite season is autumn.'

Thom M Shuman is an associate of the Iona Community and the author of *The Jesse Tree: Advent Readings* (Wild Goose Publications).

Josie Smith has been a teacher, a freelance radio and TV broadcaster, a Methodist preacher, and worked for 13 years on the staff of the Methodist headquarters. She is now actively retired in Sheffield.

Nancy Somerville, who lives in Edinburgh, is an associate of the Iona Community. Her first poetry collection is *Waiting for Zebras* (Red Squirrel Press, Scotland), 2008.

Simon Taylor is a Baptist minister who works for Churches Together in Devon and is on the ministry team of an ecumenical church in North Plymouth. He lives on Dartmoor, as it is one of the few places in Devon where you get to make a snowman in the winter. He seeks to include images from the world around us in his prayers and liturgies.

Reinhild Traitler is a member of the Iona Community.

Rosie Watson lives in Hertfordshire with her husband but regularly travels to and from Suffolk. Contrary to expectations, she is finding her 60s full of new learning. She is still working through the experience of 10 weeks in Johannesburg (Autumn 2008): who and where God is in the paradox and AIDS, alongside Africa's enduring beauty.

Lynda Wright – After working with the Community for three years as a member of the resident group, for the last fifteen years Lynda has been engaged in the ministry of hospitality and retreat at Key House, in Falkland, Fife.

INDEX OF AUTHORS

THE IONA COMMUNITY IS:

- An ecumenical movement of men and women from different walks of life and different traditions in the Christian church
- Committed to the gospel of Jesus Christ, and to following where that leads, even into the unknown
- Engaged together, and with people of goodwill across the world, in acting, reflecting and praying for justice, peace and the integrity of creation
- Convinced that the inclusive community we seek must be embodied in the community we practise

Together with our staff, we are responsible for:

- Our islands residential centres of Iona Abbey, the MacLeod Centre on Iona, and Camas Adventure Centre on the Ross of Mull

and in Glasgow:

- The administration of the Community
- Our work with young people
- Our publishing house, Wild Goose Publications
- Our association in the revitalising of worship with the Wild Goose Resource Group

The Iona Community was founded in Glasgow in 1938 by George MacLeod, minister, visionary and prophetic witness for peace, in the context of the poverty and despair of the Depression. Its original task of rebuilding the monastic ruins of Iona Abbey became a sign of hopeful rebuilding of community in Scotland and beyond. Today, we are about 250 members, mostly in Britain, and 1500 associate members, with 1400 friends worldwide. Together and apart, 'we follow the light we have, and pray for more light'.

For information on the Iona Community contact:
The Iona Community, Fourth Floor, Savoy House, 140 Sauchiehall Street,
Glasgow G2 3DH, UK. Phone: 0141 332 6343
e-mail: admin@iona.org.uk; web: www.iona.org.uk

For enquiries about visiting Iona, please contact:
Iona Abbey, Isle of Iona, Argyll PA76 6SN, UK. Phone: 01681 700404
e-mail: ionacomm@iona.org.uk